RXpert SERIES Student's Companion

Pharmacy Law and Ethics

Rxpert SERIES
Student's Companion

Pharmacy Law and Ethics

Dr. Akhlesh K. Jain
Assistant Professor
School of Pharrmaceutical Sciences
Guru Ghasidas Central University, Bilaspur, C.G. India

Dr. Balak Das Kurmi
Associate Professor
ISF college of Pharmacy. Moga India

Pharma Med PRESS An Imprint of BSP Books Pvt. Ltd.

(TM) **PharmaMed Press**
An imprint of BSP Books Pvt. Ltd.
4-4-309/316, Giriraj Lane,
Sultan Bazar, Hyderabad - 500 095.

Pharmacy Law and Ethics
by **Dr. Akhlesh K. Jain and Dr. Balak Das Kurmi**

Disclaimer: The authors and the publishers have taken due care to provide the authentic, reliable and up to date information related to the subject. However, neither the authors nor the publisher shall be responsible for any liability for any damage caused as a result of use of this book. The respective user must check the accuracy from other sources too.

Published by:

PharmaMed Press

An imprint of BSP Books Pvt. Ltd.
4-4-309/316, Giriraj Lane, Sultan Bazar, Hyderabad - 500 095.
Phone: 040-23445688; Fax: 91+40-23445611
e-mail: info@pharmamedpress.com
www.pharmamedpress.com/pharmamedpress.net

ISBN: 978-93-49562-18-9 (Hardback)

Preface

It is our immense pleasure to bring out the "First Edition of Pharmacy Law Ethics and Theory book" which is dedicated to the students and faculty of D. Pharma. This book is designed and edited in accordance with the syllabus requirement of "Pharmacy Law Ethics and Theory" of the second year D. Pharm course in pharmacy prescribed in "Diploma of Pharmacy (D. Pharm) course regulations" by the Pharmacy Council of India. The entire book is divided into twenty one chapters.

Sincere efforts have been made to present theoretical aspects in detail for easy understanding.The major objective of this book is to provide students, with collective information about the subject in simple and lucid language.

We earnestly believe and apprehend that the brilliant budding students of Pharmacy (Diploma Program) in All Indian universities will definitely find this compilation extremely useful to provide them with sufficient deliberation, understanding, and in-depth knowledge on the subject perceptively.

We are grateful to PharmaMed Press, Hyderabad for all their efforts in publishing this book.

Suggestions and comments are always welcome and they shall be gratefully acknowledged.

- Authors

Contents

Preface .... (v)

Chapter 1

General Principles of Law, History, and Various Acts Related to Drugs and the Pharmacy Profession 1

Chapter 2

Pharmacy Act 1948 and Rules

Introduction 4

Objectives 4

Definitions 4

Registration of Pharmacist 6

Pharmacy Practise Regulation, 2015 8

Chapter 3

Drugs and Cosmetics Act 1940 and Rules 1945 and New Amendments

Definition 11

Import of Drugs and Cosmetics 12

Manufacture of Drugs 14

Schedule C 20

Schedule G 22

Schedule H 24

Schedule K 24

Schedule M 25

Schedule N 34

Schedule P 35

Schedule X 36

Sale of Drugs 40

Administration of the Act and Rules 42

Licensing Authorities 45

Government Analyst 45

Chapter 4

Narcotic Drugs and Psychotropic Substances Act 1985 and Rules

Introduction 48
Objectives 48
Definition 49
Prohibition, Control and Regulation 51

Chapter 5

Drug and Magic Remedies (Objectionable Advertisement) Act 1954

Definition 53
Objectives 53
Commencement 54
Prohibition of Certain Advertisement 54
Classes of Prohibited Advertisement 54
Classes of Prohibited Advertisement Includes 55
Offences and Penalties 58

Chapter 6

Prevention of Cruelty to Animals Act-1960

Introduction 60
Objectives 60
CPCSEA 61
Institutional Animal Ethics Committee 62
Breeding and Stocking of Animals 63
Performance of Experiments 64
Transfer and Acquisition of Animals for Experiment 65

Chapter 7

Poison Act-1919

Introduction 69
Scope 70
Objectives 70
Possession and Sale of Poisons 70
Import of Poisons 72

Chapter 8

Food Safety and Standards Authority of India (FSSAI)

Introduction 74
The Food Safety and Standards Act 2006 75

Chapter 9

DPCO

Introduction 79
Objectives 79
DPCO 2013 79
Pricing of Scheduled Formulation 81
Conclusion 82

Chapter 10

Code of Ethics

Law 83
Ethics 83
Pharmaceutical Code of Ethics 83
Pharmacist in Relation to His Job 84
Pharmacist in Relation to His Trade 85
Pharmacist in Relation to Medical Profession 86
Pharmacist in Relation to His Profession 86
Pharmacist's OTH 87

Chapter 11

Medical Termination of Pregnancy Act and Rules

Induction of Abortion 88
MTP Act: Addressing a Public Health Priority 88

Chapter 12

Government Pharma Regulatory Bodies

Role of Regulatory Bodies 91
Central Drug Standard Control Organization (CDSCO) 91
Indian Pharmacopoeia Commission (IPC) 93

Chapter 13

Good Regulatory Practices

Introduction 96
Principles of GRP 96
Licenses Required under (GRP) 98
E-governance 101

Chapter 14

Introduction to BCS System

Introduction 103
Abbreviated New Drug Application (ANDA) 104
NDA (New Drug Application) 105
Brand v/s Generic Drugs 106
Trade Name Concept 106
Emergency Use Authorization (EUA) 107

Chapter 15

Blood Bank

Introduction 109
Objective 110
Various Services Provided in a Blood Bank 110
Legal Framework Scenario 112

Chapter 16

Clinical Establishment Act and Rules

Introduction 117
National Accreditation Board for Hospitals and Healthcare Providers (NABH) Standards 118
Indian Medical Council (Professional Conduct, Etiquette, and Ethics) Regulations, 2002 119
Consumer Protection Act, 2019 119
Drugs and Cosmetics Act,1940 119
Indian Nursing Council Act, 1947 120

Chapter 17

Biomedical Waste Management Rules 2016

Introduction 122

Chapter 18

Bioethics

Introduction 127
History of Bioethics 127
Principle of Bioethics 128
Indian Council of Medical Research (ICMR) 129

Chapter 19

Introduction to Consumer Protection Act

Introduction 133
How to File a Complaint? 135

Chapter 20

Introduction to Disaster Management Act

Introduction 137
Role of Pharmacist in Disaster Management 139

Chapter 21

Medical Devices

Introduction 141
Classification of Medical Devices 142
Basic Aspects Related to Manufacture and Sale 142

CHAPTER 1

General Principles of Law, History, and Various Acts Related to Drugs and the Pharmacy Profession

Pharmacy, a vital healthcare profession, encompasses the preparation and dispensing of medicinal drugs, with pharmacists playing a pivotal role in ensuring the safe and effective use of medications. This multifaceted profession spans drug discovery, development, manufacturing, distribution, and patient care. The field of pharmaceutical sciences integrates chemistry, biology, pharmacology, and technology to discover, develop, and manufacture drugs. The meticulous process of drug development involves scientific research, beginning with the identification of potential drug targets and extending to the formulation of pharmaceutical products. Medicinal chemists design molecules with desired therapeutic effects, utilizing computational modeling and structure-activity relationship studies to optimize efficacy and safety. Preclinical testing assesses safety profiles and pharmacokinetics before drugs enter clinical trials. Clinical pharmacy, a specialized field, prioritizes patient care, medication management, and therapeutic outcome optimization, with pharmacists collaborating within healthcare teams. The legal and regulatory framework surrounding pharmacy aims to ensure public health safety, covering aspects such as drug approval, labeling, and controlled substance handling. Regulatory agencies, including the Food and Drug Administration (FDA), set rigorous standards. Pharmacists navigate a complex web of federal, state, and local regulations, crucial for maintaining professional integrity and patient trust. Pharmacy practice, bound not only by laws but also ethical principles, requires pharmacists to address ethical dilemmas, uphold patient autonomy and confidentiality, and prioritize patient well-being while complying with legal requirements. The historical evolution of pharmacy, from ancient civilizations to modern standardization, and the legal foundations of the profession contribute to a comprehensive understanding within the broader healthcare regulatory context. The historical perspective of pharmacy practices traces back to ancient civilizations such as Egypt, Mesopotamia, and China, where early pharmaceutical knowledge was evident in medical recipes and prescriptions. The Middle Ages witnessed the pivotal role of monasteries and the emergence of apothecaries, marking a transition to more scientific approaches during the Renaissance. The 19th century saw scientific advancements, leading to the isolation of active compounds and the industrialization of drug manufacturing. Concurrently, the formation of professional organizations contributed to the modernization and standardization of pharmacy. Regarding the general principles of law in pharmacy, constitutional considerations include the Commerce Clause, due process, and the Supremacy Clause. Federal laws like the Food, Drug, and Cosmetic Act (FDCA) and the Controlled Substances Act (CSA) empower regulatory bodies such as the FDA and DEA, while each state maintains its Pharmacy Practice Act. A comprehension of this historical evolution and legal foundation is crucial for contextualizing the pharmacy profession within the broader scope of healthcare regulation. Constitutional considerations, such as due process and equal protection, form the basis for fair treatment and non-discrimination in the field. At the federal level, laws like the Controlled Substances Act (CSA) and the Food, Drug, and Cosmetic Act (FDCA) regulate drug manufacturing, distribution, and safety. Regulatory agencies, including the Food and Drug Administration (FDA) overseeing drug approval and the Drug Enforcement Administration (DEA) monitoring controlled substances, play pivotal roles. State Pharmacy Boards regulate licensing and professional conduct, with compliance checks, inspections, and penalties ensuring adherence to legal frameworks. Pharmacists must be vigilant in navigating these legal intricacies, ensuring compliance to maintain their professional status and safeguard patient welfare in an ever-evolving regulatory landscape. The Food, Drug, and Cosmetic Act (FDCA), instituted in 1938, serves as the bedrock for regulating food, drugs, and cosmetics, emphasizing safety, efficacy, and proper labeling. The Controlled Substances Act (CSA), enacted in 1970, meticulously oversees controlled substances, categorizing them by abuse potential and mandating strict regulations enforced by the Drug Enforcement Administration (DEA). The Drug Price Competition and Patent Term Restoration Act (Hatch-Waxman Act) of 1984 encourages generic drug competition while preserving patent incentives for innovation. Additionally, the Drug Enforcement and Abuse Prevention Acts, encompassing various amendments, address contemporary challenges, especially in combating opioid abuse through enhanced regulations and monitoring programs. These acts collectively establish a robust legal framework, shaping the pharmaceutical landscape and guiding pharmacy practices to ensure public safety, access to medications, and fair competition. The discussion further highlights the dynamic nature of these regulations and their tangible impact on daily pharmacy operations and patient care. Pharmacy Practice Acts, integral to the regulatory fabric of each state, meticulously define the parameters within which pharmacists and pharmacy technicians operate. These acts encompass the entire spectrum of pharmacy practice, from licensing and registration requirements to outlining the scope of professional responsibilities. Addressing nuances such as continuing education mandates, they underscore the commitment to ongoing professional development for pharmacists. The acts also establish stringent licensing processes, renewal criteria, and disciplinary measures to ensure the highest standards of competence and ethical conduct within the profession. Navigating through the intricacies of state-specific regulations, professionals grapple with variations, making it imperative to stay vigilant about changes. As the pharmacy landscape evolves, these acts face the challenge of adapting to technological advancements, with considerations for tele-pharmacy and other emerging trends. Overall, Pharmacy Practice Acts not only safeguard public health by maintaining the integrity of pharmaceutical services but also shape the trajectory of the pharmacy profession within the dynamic framework of each state. Beginning with an exploration of the legal foundations, the discussion encompasses patient privacy and confidentiality, elucidating the pharmacist's responsibilities in safeguarding sensitive information and the potential repercussions of breaches. Informed consent is thoroughly examined, emphasizing effective communication strategies employed by pharmacists to ensure patients comprehend the nuances of their medications. The segment also delves into the professional code of conduct, illuminating key ethical principles embedded in codes such as those established by organizations like the American Pharmacists Association. Practical application is emphasized through real-world examples, while a forward-looking perspective addresses potential future challenges, offering a holistic view of ethical considerations crucial for pharmacists to navigate the complexities of their profession with integrity and professionalism.

CHAPTER 2

Pharmacy Act 1948 and Rules

Introduction

The Drugs Enquiry Committee and Health Survey and Development Committee's recommendations laid the foundation for enacting the Pharmacy Act, of 1948. The Act was established to regulate the pharmacy profession in India and has five chapters and 46 sections. In 1976, an amendment was made to Section 42 of the Act, which mandates that registered pharmacists must supervise drug stores in the country. The Pharmacy Act, of 1948 is divided into five chapters. Chapter I and Chapter II, which deal with introductory and the Pharmacy Council of India (PCI), respectively, come into effect immediately. The Pharmacy Council of India was established in 1949. Chapter III, Chapter IV, and Chapter V, which deal with the State Pharmacy Council (SPC), Registration of Pharmacists, and Miscellaneous, respectively, were implemented within a specific timeframe.

Objectives

- Improve the status of the profession of pharmacy.
- Provide uniform education and training.
- Maintain control over the pharmacy profession.
- Regulate the pharmacy practice.
- Restore the pharmacy profession.

Definitions

A registered Medical Practitioner (RMP) is a healthcare professional who has a recognized medical qualification as defined in clause (h) of section 2 of the Indian Medical Council Act, 1956 (102 of 1956), whose name has been entered in a State Medical Register, and who has experience or training in gynecology and obstetrics as prescribed by Rules under this Act. A Registered Pharmacist is a person who is registered as a pharmacist and whose name is currently entered in the register of the state.

Pharmacy Council of India

Ex- Officio Members	Elected Members	Nominates Members
The Director-General of Medical and Health Services, Government of India, or his/her nominee is a position of authority in the Indian healthcare system.	The PCI comprises six members, at least one of whom is a teacher of each of the subjects of Pharmacy, elected by the University Grants Commission from among teachers at Indian Universities or affiliated colleges imparting diplomas or degrees in pharmacy.	The PCI is composed of six members nominated by the Government of India Ministry of Health and Family Welfare, of which at least four should possess a degree or diploma in pharmacy qualification and should be practicing pharmacy or pharmaceutical chemistry.
The Drugs Controller General of India (DCGI) is the head of the Central Drugs Standard Control Organization (CDSCO) of the Government of India. The DCGI is responsible for approving licenses of specified categories of drugs such as blood and blood products, IV fluids, vaccines, and sera in India	One member elected from amongst its members of the Medical Council of India" means that one member will be chosen from the Medical Council of India to represent the council.	One representative each of University Grants Commission (UGC) and All India Council for Technical Education (AICTE)" means that one member will be chosen from the University Grants Commission and one member will be chosen from the All-India Council for Technical Education to represent their respective organizations.
Oversees the Central Drugs Laboratory located in Kolkata, India. The laboratory is responsible for the quality control of drugs and cosmetics in India and is established under the Indian Drugs & Cosmetics Act, of 1940. It is the oldest quality control laboratory of the Drug Control Authorities in India and functions under the administrative control of the Director-General of Health Services in the Ministry of Health and Family Welfare	The statement "One member each elected by the State Pharmacy Council of each State who should be a registered pharmacist" can be rephrased as "Each State Pharmacy Council elects one member who is a registered pharmacist".	The statement "One member representing each State Government or Union Territory who shall be a registered pharmacist nominated by the respective State Government or Union Territory" can be rephrased as "Each State Government or Union Territory nominates one registered pharmacist as their representtative.

Functions of PCI

1. ER prescribes the minimum qualifications for registration and admission, duration of training during the course, syllabus, and conditions to be fulfilled by the institute and university.
2. ER is responsible for regulating the ER in the states.
3. Approval of the institute is granted under Section 12 of the Pharmacy Act, 1948 after the infrastructure facility is examined by an inspector.

4. Approval can be withdrawn if the guidelines of ER are not followed.
5. Recognition of other qualifications is granted if anyone is qualified by an authority outside India.
6. ER is responsible for the preparation and maintenance of the central register of pharmacists.
7. ER fixes the rate of allowance of its members.
8. ER decides the mode of election.

Pharmacy Council

State Pharmacy Council	Joint State Pharmacy Council
I Elected Members	
The State Pharmacy Council includes both elected and nominated representatives to oversee matters related to pharmacy practice and regulation.	The State Pharmacy Council includes 3 to 5 members who are elected from among registered pharmacists in each participating state12. These elected members play a crucial role in overseeing pharmacy-related matters within their respective states.
The one member, who is a registered medical practitioner, is elected by the Medical Council of the State and represents the medical profession within the state and contributes to decision-making and governance related to medical practice and regulations.	The one member, who is a registered medical practitioner, is elected by the Medical Council of each participating State. This individual represents the medical profession within the state and contributes to decision-making and governance related to medical practice and regulations.
II Nominated Members	
Each state nominates five members, with a requirement that at least three of them hold degrees or diplomas in pharmacy or pharmaceutical chemistry.	From each participating state, 2 to 4 members are nominated, with a requirement that more than 50% of them hold degrees or diplomas in pharmacy or pharmaceutical chemistry.
III Ex-Officio Members	
The Chief Administrative Officer or the In charge of Medical and Health Services for each state, or their nominee.	The Chief Administrative Officer or the In charge of Medical and Health Services for each participating state, or their nominee.
The Officer In charge is responsible for enforcing the Drugs and Cosmetic Act, of 1940 in each state, or their nominee.	The Officer In charge responsible for enforcing the Drugs and Cosmetic Act, 1940 in each participating state, or their nominee."
A Government Analyst, nominated by the State Government under the Drugs and Cosmetics Act, of 1940.	Each participating state nominates one Government Analyst under the Drugs and Cosmetics Act (DCA) of 1940.

Registration of Pharmacist

First Register of Pharmacists

- Established immediately after India's independence until the State Pharmacy Council (SPC) was constituted.
- Due to a shortage of pharmacists, State Governments formed a Registration Tribunal comprising three members, with one acting as Secretary-cum-Treasurer.

Eligibility criteria included

- Minimum age of 18 years.
- Approved Chemist and Druggist diploma certificate.
- Graduation in any discipline with at least three years of experience in compounding and dispensing.

Subsequent Register

It was created during the period of implementing the Pharmacy Act and framing educational regulations.

During the period before Education Regulations were fully implemented in the State, eligible candidates' names were added to the pharmacist register based on the following criteria:

- Minimum age of 18 years
- A person meeting conditions approved by the Central Council or conditions that allow entry into the first register, provided they hold a matriculate qualification.
- Alternatively, a person with a matriculate qualification who is already a registered pharmacist in another State.

Regular Register

- Established after Education Regulations came into force.
- After the implementation of Education Regulations framed by the Pharmacy Council of India, only individuals holding a diploma in pharmacy from an institution approved by the PCI are eligible for registration as pharmacists.
- Qualify, they must have completed practical training of five hundred hours after finishing their D. Pharm. course.

The State Pharmacy Council maintains an up-to-date register of pharmacists, which includes the following details:

- Full Name and residential address of the pharmacist.
- Date of first admission to the Register or Date of Registration.
- Qualification and year of passing the qualifying examination.
- Professional address.
- Date of Birth and any other relevant particulars as prescribed.

Removal of Name from Register (Sec-36)

- A person whose name has been mistakenly entered in the Register due to an error or misrepresentation.
- Someone who provides false information about themselves.

- An individual who submits fraudulent certificates or documents in support of their registration.
- A person convicted of an offense related to their profession.
- Someone indirectly involved in a professional offense, where it is proven that they instigated or connived at the offense committed by a registered pharmacist.

Offences and Penalties

- Section 42 of the Act prohibits anyone other than a registered pharmacist from compounding, preparing, mixing, or dispensing medicine based on a medical practitioner's prescription.
- Violating this provision can result in imprisonment of six months or a fine of Rs. 1000.00, or both.
- Additionally, falsely claiming to be a registered pharmacist carries a penalty of Rs. 500.00 for the first conviction and imprisonment of up to six months or a fine of Rs. 1000.00, or both, for subsequent convictions.

Pharmacy Practice Regulation, 2015

Practice of Pharmacy

- Interpreting and implementing medical orders, including dispensing prescriptions and drug orders.
- Dispensing, compounding, and administering drugs.
- Participating in drug and device selection and conducting drug-related research.
- Providing patient counseling, delivering patient care, and practicing pharmaceutical care.

Patient Counselling

Patient Counselling involves oral communication by pharmacists to patients or caregivers, providing information about the proper use of drugs and drug devices.

Pharmaceutical Care

Pharmaceutical Care is a patient-centred practice where pharmacists take responsibility for addressing patients' drug-related needs, aiming to prevent, eliminate, or reduce symptoms and diseases.

Pharmacy Practitioner

An individual currently licensed, registered or authorized under the Pharmacy Act to counsel or administer drugs to patients.

- **Community Pharmacist:** Supply prescription medicines and provides advice and information on people's health.

- **Hospital Pharmacist:** Dispensing of drugs to the patients and advise them about medicines.

Clinical Pharmacist

These professionals focus on patient care, ensuring optimal medication use, and promoting health, wellness, and disease prevention. They collaborate closely with physicians and other healthcare providers.

Drug Information Pharmacist

Their role involves providing advice on drug interactions, side effects, proper dosages, and appropriate medication storage to patients and other healthcare professionals.

Code of Pharmacy Ethics

- **Patient Care:** Pharmacists prioritize patient well-being.
- **Honesty and Trustworthiness:** Uphold ethical standards.
- **Responsibility:** Be accountable to colleagues and other healthcare professionals.
- **Continuous Learning:** Stay updated and competent in professional knowledge.
- **Respect and Confidentiality:** Support patients' individuality, dignity, and confidentiality.
- **Record Keeping:** Maintain accurate patient records.
- **Ethical Conduct:** Avoid illegal or unethical behaviour that discredits the profession.
- **Prohibition:** Renting or leasing a Pharmacy Registration Certificate is strictly prohibited.

Displaying the name of Owner and Registered Pharmacist

- **Registered Pharmacist Display:** The name of a registered pharmacist should be prominently displayed at the main entrance of the premises or building.
- **Sign Board Information:** Registered pharmacists may exhibit their name, educational qualifications, registration number, and photograph on a signboard.
- **Professional Attire:** While working, pharmacists should wear a clean white apron with a badge plate that includes their name and registration number.

Good Pharmacy Practise

- **Association Membership:** Joining professional associations contributes to the advancement of the pharmacy profession and is part of ongoing pharmacy education.
- **Patient Records Maintenance:** Pharmacists must maintain patient records for at least 5 years from the start of treatment, preferably in a computerized format for efficient retrieval.
- **Unethical Conduct Exposure:** Pharmacists should expose income-petence, corruption, and dishonest or unethical behavior.
- **Quality Assurance:** By doing so, they help safeguard the profession against individuals lacking moral character or education.

Renewal of Registration

To renew their registration, pharmacists must participate in at least two refresher courses within 5 years. These courses are organized by various entities, including the Pharmacy Council of India, State Pharmacy Councils, Central Government, and recognized professional bodies. These educational programs help pharmacists stay updated and maintain their competence in the field.

Pharmaceutical Care

- Only Registered Pharmacists are authorized to perform the following actions to ensure therapeutic appropriateness:
- Identify overutilization or underutilization of medications.
- Recognize therapeutic duplication.
- Assess drug-release interactions.
- Detect incorrect drug dosages or durations.
- Consider drug-allergy interactions.
- Correlate drug availability.
- Address clinical abuse or misuse.

When any of these issues are recognized, the Registered Pharmacist must take appropriate steps to prevent or resolve the problem.

CHAPTER 3

Drugs and Cosmetics Act 1940 and Rules 1945 and New Amendments

The Drugs and Cosmetics Act, 1940 is a crucial part of legislation enacted by the Indian Parliament. Its purpose is to regulate the import, manufacture, and distribution of medicines within the country. The act aims to ensure that drugs and cosmetics sold in India meet stringent safety, efficacy, and quality standards. Additionally, the Drugs and Cosmetics Rules, 1945 complement this act by providing detailed guidelines for the classification of drugs into specific schedules. These rules cover aspects such as storage, sale, display, and prescription for each category of drugs. The Drugs and Cosmetics Act of 1940, as per the provided excerpt, specifies its short title, extent, and commencement. The Act, known as the Drugs and Cosmetics Act, 1940, applies across the entirety of India. It comes into effect immediately upon enactment. However, Chapter III of the Act will only become operational from a date specified by the Central Government through notification in the Official Gazette. Similarly, Chapter IV of the Act will take effect in a particular State from a date specified by the State Government through a similar notification. Notably, for the State of Jammu and Kashmir, the commencement of Chapter III will occur after the Central Government specifies a date following the commencement of the Drugs and Cosmetics (Amendment) Act, 1972, through notification in the Official Gazette.

Definition

In this Act, unless the subject or context requires otherwise, the term "Ayurvedic, Siddha or Unani drug" encompasses all medications intended for internal or external use in diagnosing, treating, mitigating, or preventing diseases or disorders in humans or animals. These drugs are manufactured exclusively following the formulas outlined in the authoritative texts of Ayurvedic, Siddha, and Unani Tibb systems of medicine specified in the First Schedule. Furthermore, "the Board" refers to two distinct entities: firstly, concerning Ayurvedic, Siddha, or Unani drugs, it denotes the Ayurvedic, Siddha, and Unani Drugs Technical Advisory Board established under section 33C; secondly, regarding any other drug or cosmetic, it signifies the Drugs Technical Advisory Board formed under section 5.

Import of Drugs and Cosmetics

1. **Standards of quality:** the purposes outlined in this Chapter; the term "standard quality" signifies the following:
   (a) Concerning a drug, it denotes that the drug meets the standard specified in the Second Schedule.
   (b) Regarding a cosmetic, it indicates that the cosmetic conforms to the standard prescribed by regulations. The Central Government, following consultation with the Board and after providing not less than three months' notice of its intention through notification in the Official Gazette, holds the authority to append to or modify the Second Schedule, pertaining to this Chapter, through a similar notification. Subsequently, the Second Schedule will be considered amended accordingly.
2. **Misbranded drugs:** For the purposes delineated in this Chapter, a drug shall be considered misbranded under the following circumstances:(a) If its color, coating, powdering, or polishing conceals damage or if it is presented to appear to possess a therapeutic value superior to its actual properties.(b) If it lacks labeling in the prescribed manner.(c) If any statement, design, or device on its label, container, or accompanying materials presents false claims or is misleading regarding the drug's attributes or efficacy.

   2A. Adulterated drugs: In this Chapter, a drug shall be considered adulterated under the following conditions:(a) If it includes, wholly or partially, any filthy, putrid, or decomposed substance.(b) If it has been prepared, packaged, or stored under unsanitary conditions that could lead to contamination with filth or render it harmful to health.(c) If its container comprises, wholly or partly, any poisonous or deleterious substance that could render the contents harmful to health.(d) If it bears or contains a color, solely for coloring purposes, other than the one prescribed.(e) If it contains any harmful or toxic substance that could render it harmful to health.(f) If any substance has been added to it to diminish its quality or potency.

   2B. Spurious drugs: For the purposes outlined in this Chapter, a drug shall be considered spurious under the following circumstances:(a)If it is imported under a name that corresponds to another drug.(b) If it imitates, substitutes, or resembles another drug in a manner likely to deceive, or if it bears the name of another drug on its label or container without being clearly marked to reveal its true identity.(c) If the label or container displays the name of an individual or company purportedly manufacturing the drug, and such individual or company is either fictitious or non-existent.(d) If it has been wholly or partially replaced by another drug or substance.(e) If it claims to be the product of a manufacturer when it is not genuinely produced by that manufacturer.

2C. Misbranded cosmetics: For the purposes outlined in this chapter, a cosmetic shall be deemed misbranded under the following circumstances:(a) If it contains a color not prescribed. (b) If it lacks labeling in the prescribed manner.(c) If the label, container, or any accompanying material contains a statement that is false or misleading in any aspect.

2D. Spurious cosmetics: For the purposes outlined in this Chapter, a drug shall be considered spurious under the following conditions:(a) If it is imported under a name belonging to another cosmetic. (b) If it imitates, substitutes, or resembles another cosmetic in a manner likely to deceive, or if it bears the name of another cosmetic on its label or container without being plainly or conspicuously marked to reveal its true character and its lack of identity with such other cosmetic. (c) If the label or container bears the name of an individual or company purporting to be the manufacturer of the cosmetic, and such individual or company is fictitious or non-existent.(d) If it claims to be the product of a manufacturer when it is not genuinely produced by that manufacturer.

3. Prohibition of import of certain drugs or cosmetics: From a date determined by the Central Government through notification in the Official Gazette, the import of certain drugs or cosmetics is prohibited:(a) Drugs or cosmetics that do not meet standard quality requirements.(b) Misbranded drugs or misbranded or spurious cosmetics; adulterated or spurious drugs.(c) Drugs or cosmetics requiring a prescribed license for import, unless imported under such license.(d) Patent or proprietary medicines without displaying the true formula or list of active ingredients on the label or container as prescribed.(e) Drugs claiming to cure or mitigate diseases or ailments beyond prescribed limits.(f) Drugs or cosmetics whose import is prohibited by rules under this Chapter. However, exceptions exist for the import, under specified conditions, of small quantities of drugs for examination, test, analysis, or personal use. Moreover, the Central Government, following consultation with the Board, may permit, under prescribed conditions, the import of drugs or drug classes not meeting standard quality requirements, as specified in the notification.

3A. Power of Central Government to prohibit the import of drugs and cosmetics in the public interest: The Central Government, regardless of other provisions within this Chapter, holds the authority to prohibit the import of any drug or cosmetic if it deems that its usage may pose risks to humans or animals, or if the drug lacks the claimed therapeutic value or contains ingredients in quantities without therapeutic justification. In the interest of public welfare, the Government may issue a notification in the Official Gazette to enforce such prohibition.

Manufacture of Drugs

Any process or part of a process for making, altering, ornamenting, finishing, packing, labelling, breaking up or otherwise treating or adopting any drug or cosmetic with a view to its sale or distribution but does not include the compounding or dispensing of any drug, or the packing of any drug or cosmetic, in the ordinary course of retail business; and "to manufacture" shall be construed accordingly.

Prohibition of Manufacture and Sale of Certain Drugs

In many countries, including India, there are laws that prohibit the manufacture and sale of certain drugs. These laws are typically in place to regulate the production, distribution, and use of substances that are deemed harmful, addictive, or pose a significant risk to public health and safety. For example, in India, the Drugs and Cosmetics Act, 1940, and its associated rules regulate the manufacture, sale, and distribution of drugs. Under this act, certain drugs are classified as "scheduled drugs" or "prohibited drugs." The manufacture, sale, or distribution of these prohibited drugs is strictly prohibited, and violations can lead to severe penalties, including fines and imprisonment.

The specifics of which drugs are prohibited can vary from one jurisdiction to another and may include substances such as narcotics, psychotropic substances, and other controlled substances. These laws are typically enforced by government regulatory agencies, such as the Central Drugs Standard Control Organization (CDSCO) in India, along with law enforcement authorities. It's important for individuals and businesses involved in the manufacture and sale of drugs to be aware of these laws and comply with their provisions to avoid legal consequences. Additionally, these laws may be periodically updated or amended to address emerging concerns or changes in public health priorities.

Conditions for the Grant of a License

The manufacture of drugs varies depending on the country and its specific regulations:

1. **Compliance with Regulations:** Applicants for a manufacturing license must demonstrate compliance with all relevant laws, regulations, and guidelines pertaining to drug manufacturing. This includes adherence to Good Manufacturing Practices (GMP) or similar standards established by regulatory authorities.

2. **Premises and Facilities:** The manufacturing facility must meet certain standards for cleanliness, sanitation, and suitability for drug production. This may involve specific requirements for equipment, storage areas, production areas, and utilities.
3. **Technical Personnel:** The applicant must have qualified technical personnel responsible for overseeing the manufacturing process. This may include individuals with appropriate educational qualifications and experience in pharmaceutical manufacturing.
4. **Quality Control:** Adequate provisions must be in place for quality control testing of raw materials, intermediates, and finished products. This includes the availability of testing facilities, equipment, and trained personnel.
5. **Documentation and Record-Keeping:** The applicant must maintain comprehensive documentation and records related to the manufacturing process, including batch records, quality control records, and standard operating procedures (SOPs).
6. **Product Registration:** For certain types of drugs, the applicant may need to obtain product registration or marketing authorization from the regulatory authority before commencing manufacturing.
7. **Safety and Environmental Standards:** The manufacturing process must be conducted in a manner that ensures the safety of personnel, as well as environmental protection. This may involve compliance with occupational health and safety regulations and environmental regulations.
8. **Inspections and Audits:** Regulatory authorities may conduct inspections or audits of the manufacturing facility to verify compliance with licensing requirements. Applicants must cooperate with such inspections and address any deficiencies identified by regulatory inspectors.

Manufacturing Drugs for Testing Purposes

It involves specific regulations and procedures to ensure safety, efficacy, and compliance with regulatory requirements. The general steps and considerations involved in manufacturing drugs for testing are as follows:

1. **Regulatory Approval:** Before initiating drug manufacturing for testing purposes, the manufacturer typically needs to obtain regulatory approval or authorization from the relevant authorities. This may involve submitting an application, providing documentation regarding the intended use of the drugs, and obtaining any necessary permits or licenses.
2. **Good Manufacturing Practices (GMP):** Manufacturers must adhere to Good Manufacturing Practices (GMP) or similar quality standards established by regulatory authorities. GMP guidelines ensure that drugs

are consistently produced and controlled according to quality standards appropriate for their intended use.

3. **Quality Control:** Manufacturers must establish quality control measures to ensure the quality, purity, and potency of the drugs being manufactured for testing. This includes testing raw materials, intermediates, and finished products for compliance with specifications and standards.
4. **Documentation and Record-Keeping:** Comprehensive documentation and record-keeping are essential throughout the manufacturing process. This includes maintaining batch records, manufacturing protocols, testing results, and other relevant documentation to demonstrate compliance with regulatory requirements.
5. **Labeling and Packaging:** Drugs manufactured for testing purposes must be appropriately labeled and packaged to ensure identification, traceability, and safety. Labels should include necessary information such as product name, strength, dosage form, expiration date, and cautionary statements.
6. **Safety Considerations:** Manufacturers must prioritize safety considerations during drug manufacturing for testing. This includes ensuring the safety of personnel involved in the manufacturing process, as well as implementing measures to prevent cross-contamination and environmental hazards.
7. **Ethical Considerations:** Manufacturers should adhere to ethical principles and guidelines when manufacturing drugs for testing, particularly if human subjects are involved in clinical trials or studies. This includes obtaining informed consent, protecting participant confidentiality, and ensuring that testing protocols adhere to ethical standards.
8. **Compliance with Regulations:** Throughout the manufacturing process, manufacturers must comply with all relevant laws, regulations, and guidelines governing drug manufacturing and testing. This includes regulations related to drug safety, efficacy, labeling, packaging, and distribution.

Examination and Analysis of Drugs

Examination and analysis are critical steps in ensuring quality, safety, and efficacy of drugs. These processes involve various techniques and procedures to assess the physical, chemical, and biological properties of drugs.

1. **Physical Examination:** This involves visual inspection and examination of the physical characteristics of drugs, including their appearance, color, odor, texture, and physical form (e.g., solid, liquid, or semi-solid). Physical examination helps identify any abnormalities, such as discoloration, foreign particles, or physical defects.

2. **Chemical Analysis:** Chemical analysis involves determining the chemical composition and identity of drugs. Techniques such as chromatography (e.g., high-performance liquid chromatography, gas chromatography), spectroscopy (e.g., infrared spectroscopy, ultraviolet-visible spectroscopy), and mass spectrometry are commonly used for chemical analysis. Chemical analysis helps confirm the presence of active pharmaceutical ingredients (APIs), assess purity, and detect impurities or degradation products.
3. **Quantitative Analysis:** Quantitative analysis involves determining the quantity or concentration of drugs and their components. This includes assay methods to quantify the amount of the active pharmaceutical ingredient (API) present in a drug formulation, as well as the determination of related substances, impurities, and degradation products.
4. **Microbiological Testing:** Microbiological testing assesses the microbial quality and sterility of drugs. This includes tests for microbial contamination, such as total viable count, tests for specific pathogens, and sterility testing to ensure that drugs are free from viable microorganisms.
5. **Stability Testing:** Stability testing evaluates the chemical and physical stability of drugs over time under various environmental conditions (e.g., temperature, humidity, light). This helps assess the shelf-life of drugs and ensure that they maintain their quality, potency, and efficacy throughout their intended storage period.
6. **Dissolution Testing:** Dissolution testing measures the rate and extent of drug release from solid dosage forms (e.g., tablets, capsules) in simulated physiological conditions. Dissolution testing helps assess the drug's bioavailability and performance characteristics, particularly for orally administered drugs.
7. **Biological Testing:** Biological testing involves assessing the biological activity and pharmacological effects of drugs using in vitro and in vivo models. This includes studies to evaluate efficacy, safety, pharmacokinetics, and toxicology of drugs in preclinical and clinical settings.
8. **Quality Control Testing:** Quality control testing encompasses all the above-mentioned testing procedures to ensure that drugs meet predefined quality standards and specifications. Quality control testing is conducted throughout the drug development and manufacturing process to maintain consistency and compliance with regulatory requirements.

Manufacture of a New Drug

Critical steps to ensure its safety, efficacy, and quality. Typical process involved in manufacturing a new drug:

1. **Discovery and Development:** The process begins with the discovery and development of a new drug candidate. This often involves extensive research in laboratory settings to identify compounds with potential therapeutic effects against a specific disease or condition.
2. **Preclinical Studies:** Before moving to human trials, preclinical studies are conducted to evaluate the safety, pharmacokinetics, and pharmacodynamics of the drug candidate in laboratory animals or in vitro models. These studies provide essential data to support the progression of the drug candidate to clinical trials.
3. **Clinical Trials:** Clinical trials are conducted in phases to assess the safety and efficacy of the drug candidate in human subjects. Phase I trials focus on safety and dosage escalation, Phase II trials evaluate efficacy and optimal dosing, and Phase III trials assess effectiveness and monitor side effects in larger populations. Data from clinical trials are submitted to regulatory authorities for approval.
4. **Regulatory Approval:** Once clinical trials are completed and sufficient data are gathered to demonstrate safety and efficacy, the drug developer submits a New Drug Application (NDA) or Marketing Authorization Application (MAA) to regulatory authorities (such as the FDA in the United States or the EMA in Europe) for approval to market the new drug.
5. **Manufacturing Process Development:** Concurrently with clinical development, the manufacturing process for the new drug is developed and optimized. This includes selecting appropriate raw materials, defining manufacturing processes, establishing quality control procedures, and ensuring compliance with Good Manufacturing Practices (GMP) regulations.
6. **Scale-Up and Validation:** Once the manufacturing process is developed, it undergoes scale-up to produce larger quantities of the drug for commercial distribution. Scale-up involves optimizing manufacturing parameters and ensuring consistency and quality. Validation studies are conducted to demonstrate that the manufacturing process consistently produces a product that meets predetermined specifications.
7. **Commercial Manufacturing:** Following regulatory approval, commercial manufacturing of the new drug begins. This involves large-scale production of the drug according to validated manufacturing processes and quality control procedures. Batch records are maintained,

and quality control testing is conducted to ensure product quality and consistency.

8. **Post-Marketing Surveillance:** After the new drug is launched in the market, post-marketing surveillance is conducted to monitor its safety and effectiveness in real-world settings. Adverse events and other safety concerns are monitored and reported to regulatory authorities as necessary.

In the pharmaceutical industry, a loan license and a repacking license are two different types of licenses that allow companies to engage in specific activities related to the manufacturing and distribution of pharmaceutical products.

Loan License

- A loan license is a type of manufacturing license that allows a company (the licensee) to manufacture pharmaceutical products on behalf of another company (the licensor). The licensor typically owns the product formulation and grants the license to the licensee to manufacture the product using their formulation and brand name.
- The licensee is responsible for the actual manufacturing process, including sourcing raw materials, production, quality control, and packaging, while the licensor retains ownership of the product formulation and brand.
- Loan licensing arrangements are common in the pharmaceutical industry, particularly when a company wants to expand its manufacturing capacity or leverage the manufacturing expertise of another company without investing in its own manufacturing facilities.

Repacking License

- A repacking license allows a company to repack bulk quantities of pharmaceutical products into smaller packaging for distribution or sale. This is common for products such as tablets, capsules, or liquids that are manufactured in large batches but need to be packaged into individual units or smaller quantities for retail distribution.
- The repacking process typically involves transferring the product from its original packaging (e.g., bulk containers or large bottles) into smaller packaging formats (e.g., blister packs, bottles, or sachets) suitable for retail sale or distribution to end-users.
- Companies holding repacking licenses must adhere to strict quality control standards to ensure the safety, efficacy, and integrity of the repacked products. This includes maintaining proper sanitation, labeling, and packaging practices, as well as conducting quality control testing to verify the identity, strength, and purity of the repacked products.

Schedule C

Schedule C and C1 drugs includes biological and special products. Schedule C and C1 under drug and cosmetic act & rules covers generally serum, hormones, vaccines, toxins, anti-toxins and other biological and special products.

For manufacturing for sale and distribution of Schedule C and C(1) drugs, A license on Form number 28 is required which is issued by Drug Department of concerned state government or central government. For retail sale of these drug, a license on Form 21 is required whereas for wholesale sale and distribution purpose, license on Form 21-B is required. Below is the list of products that are covered under Schedule C and C(1).

Various Form Number Required for Application of Schedule c and c1 Drugs

- **Form Number 19/19A:** Applications for the grant or renewal of a licence to sell, stock, exhibit or offer for sale or distribute drugs, other than those included in Schedule X, shall be made in Form 19 or Form 19A, as the case may be.
- **Form Number 27:** Application for grant or renewal of a licence to manufacture for sale or for distribution of drugs specified in Schedules C and C (1) excluding those specified in Part XB and Schedule X.
- **Form Number 27A:** Application for grant or renewal of a loan licence to manufacture for sale or for distribution of drugs specified in Schedules C and C(1) excluding those specified in Part XB and Schedule X.
- **Form Number 27B:** Application for grant or renewal of a licence to manufacture for sale or for distribution of drugs specified in Schedules C, C(I) and X.

Licence for Drugs Specified in Schedule c and c1 are Issued in Form

- **Form 21 [Rule 61 (2)]:** Licence to sell, stock or exhibit or offer for sale, or distribute by retail drugs specified in Schedules C and C (1) excluding those specified in Schedule X
- **Form 21A [Rule 61 (2)]:** Licence to sell, stock or exhibit or offer for sale, or distribute by retail drugs specified in Schedule C (1) excluding those specified in Schedule X for dealers who do not engage the services of a registered pharmacist
- **Form 21B [Rule 61 (2)]:** Licence to sell, stock or exhibit or offer for sale, or distribute by wholesale drugs specified in Schedules C and C (1) excluding those specified in Schedule X

- **Form 21BB [Rule 62D)]:** Licence to sell by wholesale or to distribute drugs specified in Schedule C and Schedule C (1) to the Drugs and Cosmetics Rules, 1945 from a motor vehicle
- **Form 21C [Rule 63A]:** Certificate of renewal of licence to sell, stock or exhibit or offer for sale, or distribute] drugs
- **Form 21CC [Rule 63B]:** Certificate of renewal of licence to sell, stock or exhibit or offer for sale by wholesale, or distribute] drugs from a motor vehicle
- **Form 28 [Rule 76]:** Licence to manufacture for sale or for distribution of drugs specified in Schedules C and C (1) excluding those specified in Schedule X
- **Form 28A [Rule 76-A]:** Loan Licence to manufacture for sale or for distribution of drugs specified in Schedules C and C (1) excluding those specified in Schedule X
- **Form 28B[Rule 76]:** Licence to manufacture for sale or for distribution of drugs specified in Schedules C, C(I) and X
- **Form 28D [Rule 76]:** Licence to manufacture for sale or for distribution of 2[Large Volume Parenteral/Sera and Vaccines/recombinant DNA (r-DNA) derived drugs] specified in Schedules C and C(I) excluding those specified in Schedule X.

Schedule C: Biological and Special Products

- Sera.
- Solution of serum proteins intended for injection.
- Vaccines for parenteral injections.
- Toxins.
- Antigen.
- Antitoxins.
- Neo-arsphenamine and analogous substances used for the specific treatment of infective diseases.
- Insulin.
- Pituitary (Posterior Lobe) Extract.
- Adrenaline and Solutions of Salts of Adrenaline.
- Antibiotics and preparations thereof in a form to be administered parenterally.]
- Any other preparation which is meant for parenteral administration as such or after being made up with a solvent or medium or any other sterile product and which-

- requires to be stored in a refrigerator; or
- does not require to be stored in a refrigerator.
- Sterilized surgical ligature and sterilized surgical suture.
- Bacteriophages.
- Ophthalmic preparations.
- Sterile Disposable Devices for single use only.

Schedule C (1): Other Special Products

- Drugs belonging to the Digitalis group and preparations containing drugs belonging to the Digitals group not in a form to be administered parenterally.
- Ergot and preparations containing Ergot not in a form to be administered parenterally.
- Adrenaline and preparations containing Adrenaline not in a form to be administered parenterally.
- Fish Liver Oil and preparations containing Fish Liver Oil.
- Vitamins and preparations containing any vitamins not in a form to be administered parenterally.
- Liver extract and preparations containing liver extract not in a form to be administered parenterally.
- Hormones and preparations containing Hormones not in a form to be administered parenterally.
- Vaccine not in a form to be administered parenterally.

Schedule G

- Schedule G comprises of the list of substances that are required to be used only under a medical supervision and which are to be labelled accordingly.
- Medicine listed in schedule G carries a caution in its label

  Caution: "It is dangerous to take this preparation except under medical supervision".
- Printed and surrounded by a line within which there should be no other words.
- **Conditions:**
  - ✓ The drugs that come under the preview of Schedule G drugs will simply labeled with the black colour font size in completely red colour rectangular box.

- ✓ if it contains a drug substance specified in Schedule H, be labeled with symbol Rx and conspicuously displayed on the left top corner of the label and shall also be labeled with the following words in legible black coloured font size in completely red rectangular box.
- ✓ In addition to the other particulars which are required to be printed or written under these Rules, the label of innermost container of the following categories of drugs and every other covering in which the container is packed shall bear a conspicuous red vertical line on the left side running throughout the body of the label which should not be less than 1mm in width and without disturbing the other conditions printed on the label under these rules, namely: — Narcotic analgestics, hypnotics, sedatives, tranquillisers, corticosteroids, hormones, hypoglycemics, antimicrobials, antiepileptics, antidepressants, anticoagulants, anti-cancer drugs and all other drugs falling under Schedules 'G', 'H', and 'X' whether covered or not in the above list.

List of Drugs under Schedule G

- Aminopterin
- L-Asparaginase
- Bleomycin
- Busulphan; its salts
- Carbutamide
- Chlorambucil; its salts
- Chlorothiazide and other derivatives of 1,2,4 benzothiadrazine
- Chlorpropamide; its salts
- Chlorthalidone and other derivatives of Chlorobenzene compound
- Cyclophosphomide; its salts 71a [Cytarlabine]
- Daunorubicin
- Di-Isopropyl Eluorophosphate
- Disodium Stilboestrol Diphosphate
- Doxorubicin Hydrochloride
- Ethacrynic Acid; its sats
- Ethosuximide
- Gilbenclamide
- Hydantoin; its salts, Hydroxyurea

Schedule H

This schedule contains the list of the drugs to be sold by retail only in the prescription of a registered medical practitioner (RMP).

Warning: To be sold by retail on the prescription of a Registered Medical practitioner only" prominently.

Drugs specified in Schedule H, and comes within {Narcotic Drugs and Psychotropic Substances Act, 1985} labelled with the symbol "NRx" & Schedule H drug Warning prominently.

List of Drugs Under Schedule H

Abxicimab, Acyclovir, Diclofenac, Baclofen, Carbidopa, Terazosin, etc.

Schedule K

Schedule K describe the exempted drugs, conditions and extent of exemption from all the provisions of Chapter IV of the Act and the Rules there under subject to the conditions. The drugs specified in Schedule K shall be exempted from the provisions of Chapter IV of the Act and the Rules made there under to the extent and subject to the conditions specified in that Schedule.

Exemption is provided only against fulfilment of conditions specified in Schedule.

Few Exempted Drugs are as follow:

- Drugs Labelled as 'Not for medicinal Use'.
- Quinine and other antimalarial drugs as per conditioned mention in Schedule.
- Drugs supplied by a registered medical practitioner to his own patient or any drug specified in Schedule C supplied by a registered medical practitioner at the request of another such practitioner if it is specially prepared with reference to the condition and for the use of an individual patient provided the registered medical practitioner is not (a) keeping an open shop or (b) selling across the counter or (c) engaged in the importation, manufacture, distribution or sale of all the provisions of Chapter IV of the Act and the Rules made there under, subject to the conditions mention in schedule.
- Drugs supplied by a hospital or dispensary maintained or supported by Government or local body as per conditions mentioned in schedule.
- Whole Human Blood I.P. and/or its components stored for transfusion by a First Referral Unit Community Health Centre, Primary Health Centre and Hospital as per conditions mentioned in schedule.

- Quinine Sulphate as per conditions mentioned in schedule.
- Magnesium Sulphate as per conditions mentioned in schedule.
- Some substances which are used both as articles of food as well as drugs as per conditions mentioned in schedule.
- Substances intended to be used for destruction of vermin or insects as per conditions mentioned in schedule.
- Mechanical and Chemical Contraceptives as per conditions mentioned in Schedule.
- Some household Asprin Tablets, Paracetamol Tablets, Analgesic Balms, Antacid Preparations, Gripe Water for use of infants, Inhalers, containing drugs for treatment of cold and nasal congestion, Syrups, lozenges, pills and tablets for cough, Liniments for external use, Skin ointments and ointments for burns, Absorbent cotton wool, bandages, absorbent gauze and adhesive.
- Plaster, Castor Oil, liquid Paraffin and Epsom Salt, Eucalyptus Oil, Tincture Iodine, Tincture Benzoin Co.and Mercurochrome solution in containers not exceeding 100 ml, Tablets of Quinine Sulphate I.P., Tablets of Iodochlorohydroxy quinoline – 250 mg as per conditions mentioned in schedule.
- Cosmetics as per conditions mention in schedule.
- Ophthalmic ointments of the Tetracycline group of drugs as per conditions mention in schedule.
- Hair Fixers, namely mucilagenous preparations containing gums, used by men for fixing beard as per conditions mention in schedule.
- Radio Pharmaceuticals as per conditions mentioned in schedule.
- Tablets of Chloroquine Salts as per conditions mentioned in schedule and many more.

Schedule M

The requirements of good manufacturing practices (GMP) and factory premises and the requirements of plant and equipment's.

Good Manufacturing Practices for Premises and Materials

1. **General Requirements**

   Location and surroundings: The factory building(s) for manufacture of drugs shall be so situated and shall have such measures as to avoid risk of contamination from external environment including open sewage, drain, public lavatory or any factory which produce disagreeable or obnoxious odour or fumes, excessive soot, dust, smoke, chemical or biological emissions.

Buildings and premises: The building(s) used for the factory shall be designed, constructed, adapted and maintained to suit the manufacturing operations so as to permit production of drugs under hygienic conditions. They shall conform to the conditions laid down in the Factories Act, 1948 (63 of1948).

The premises used for manufacturing, processing, warehousing, packaging, labelling and testing purposes shall be–

(i) compatible with other drug manufacturing operations that may be carried out in the same or adjacent area/ section;

(ii) adequately provided with working space to allow orderly and logical placement of equipment, material sand movement of personnel so as to:

  (a) avoid the risk of mix-up between different categories of drugs or with raw materials, intermediate sand in-process material;

  (b) avoid the possibilities of contamination and cross-contamination by providing suitable mechanism;

(iii) designed / constructed / maintained to prevent entry of insects, pests, birds, vermins and rodents. Interior surface (walls, floors and ceilings) shall be smooth and free from cracks, and permit easy cleaning, painting and disinfection

(iv) air-conditioned, where prescribed for the operations and dosage forms under production. The production and dispensing areas shall be well lighted, effectively ventilated, with air control facilities and may have proper Air Handling Units (wherever applicable) to maintain conditions including temperature and, wherever necessary, humidity, as defined for the relevant product. These conditions shall be appropriate to the category of drugs and nature of the operation. These shall also be suitable to the comforts of the personnel working with protective clothing, products handled, operations undertaken within them in relation to the external environment. These areas shall be regularly monitored for compliance with required specifications;

(v) provided with drainage system, as specified for the various categories of products, which shall be of adequate size and so designed as to prevent back- flow and/or prevent insects and rodents entering the premises. Open channels shall be avoided in manufacturing areas and, where provided, these shall be shallow to facilitate cleaning and disinfection;

(vi) the walls and floors of the areas where manufacture of drugs is carried out shall be free from cracks and open joints to avoid accumulation of dust. These shall be smooth, washable, coved and shall permit easy and effective cleaning and disinfection. The interior surfaces shall not shed particles. A periodical record of cleaning and painting of the premises shall be maintained.

Water System: There shall be valid. system for treatment of water drawn from own or any other source to render it potable in accordance with standards specified by the Bureau of Indian Standards or Local Municipality, as the case may be, so as to produce Purified Water conforming to Pharmacopoeial specification. Purified Water so produced shall only be used for all the operations except washing and cleaning operations where potable water may be used. Water shall be stored in tanks, which do not adversely affect quality of water and ensure freedom from microbiological growth. The tank shall be cleaned periodically and records maintained by the licensee in this behalf.

Disposal of waste:

(i) The disposal of sewage and effluents (solid, liquid and gas) from the manufactory shall be inconformity with the requirements of Environment Pollution Control Board.

(ii) All bio-medical waste shall be destroyed as per the provisions of the Bio- Medical Waste (Management and Handling) Rules, 1996.

(iii) Additional precautions shall be taken for the storage and disposal of rejected drugs. Records shall be maintained for all disposal of waste.

(iv) Provisions shall be made for the proper and safe storage of waste materials awaiting disposal. Hazardous, toxic substances and flammable materials shall be stored in suitably designed and segregated, enclosed are as inconformity with Central and State Legislations.

2. Warehousing Area

Adequate areas shall be designed to allow sufficient and orderly warehousing of various categories of materials and products like starting and packaging materials, intermediates, bulk and finished products, products in quarantine, released, rejected, returned or recalled, machine and equipment spare parts and change items.

Warehousing areas shall be designed and adapted to ensure good storage conditions. They shall be clean, dry and maintained with acceptable temperature limits. Where special storage conditions are required (e.g. temperature, humidity), these shall be provided, monitored and recorded. Storage are as shall have appropriate house-keeping and rodent, pests and vermin control procedures and records maintained. Proper racks, bins and platforms shall be provided for the storage of materials.

Receiving and dispatch bays shall protect materials and products from adverse weather conditions.

Where quarantine status is ensured by warehousing in separate earmarked areas in the same warehouse or store, these areas shall be clearly demarcated. Any system replacing the physical quarantine, shall give equivalent assurance of segregation. Access to these areas shall be restricted to authorized persons.

3. **Production area**

   The production area shall be designed to allow the production preferably in uni-flow and with logical sequence of operations.

   In order to avoid the risk of corss-contamination, separate dedicated and self- contained facilities shall be made available for the production of sensitive pharmaceutical products like penicillin or biological preparations with live micro-organisms. Separate dedicated facilities shall be provided for the manufacture of contamination causing and potent products such as Beta-Lactum, Sex Hormones and Cytotoxic substances.

   Working and in-process space shall be adequate to permit orderly and logical positioning of equipment and materials and movement of personnel to avoid cross- contamination and to minimize risk of omission or wrong application of any manufacturing and control measures.

   Pipe-work, electrical fittings, ventilation openings and similar service lines shall be designed, fixed and constructed to avoid 1[accumulation of dust]. Service lines shall preferably be identified by colours and the nature of the supply and direction of the flow shall be marked/indicated.

4. **Ancillary Areas**

   Rest and refreshment rooms shall be separate from other areas. These areas shall not lead directly to the manufacturing and storage areas.

   Facilities for changing, storing clothes and for washing and toilet purposes shall be easily accessible and adequate for the number of users. Toilets, separate for males and females, shall not be directly connected with production or storage areas. There shall be written instructions for cleaning and disinfection of such areas.

5. **Quality Control Area**

   Quality Control Laboratories shall be independent of the production areas. Separate areas shall be provided each for physico-chemical, biological, microbiological or radio-isotope analysis. Separate instrument room with adequate area shall be provided for sensitive and sophisticated instruments employed or analysis.

Quality Control Laboratories shall be designed appropriately for the operations to be carried out in them. Adequate space shall be provided to avoid mix-ups and cross-contamination. Sufficient and suitable storage space shall be provided for test samples, retained samples, reference standards, reagents and records.

The design of the laboratory shall take into account the suitability of construction materials and ventilation. Separate air handling units and other requirements shall be provided for biological, microbiological and radioisotopes testing areas. The laboratory shall be provided with regular supply of water of appropriate quality for cleaning and testing purposes.

Quality Control Laboratory shall be divided into separate sections i.e. for chemical, microbiological and wherever required, biological testing. These shall have adequate area for basic installation and for

Ancillary purposes. The microbiology section shall have arrangements such as air locks and laminar air flow work station, wherever considered necessary.

6. Personnel

The manufacture shall be conducted under the direct supervision of competent technical staff with prescribed qualifications and practical experience in the relevant dosage form and / or active pharmaceutical products.

The head of the Quality Control Laboratory shall be independent of the manufacturing unit. The testing shall be conducted under the direct supervision of competent technical staff who shall be whole time employees of the licensee.

Personnel for Quality Assurance and Quality Control operations shall be suitably qualified and experienced.

7. Health, clothing and sanitation of workers

The personnel handling Beta-lactum antibiotics shall be tested for Penicillin sensitivity before employment and those handling sex hormones, cytotoxic substances and other potent drugs shall be periodically examined for adverse effects. These personnel should be moved out of these sections (except in dedicated facilities), by rotation, as a health safeguard.

Prior to employment, all personnel, shall undergo medical examination including eye examination, and shall be free from Tuberculosis, skin and other communicable or contagious diseases. Thereafter, they should be medically examined periodically, at least once a year. Records shall be maintained thereof. The licensee shall provide the services of a qualified physician for assessing the health status of personnel involved in different activities.

All employees shall be instructed to report about their illness or abnormal health condition to their immediate supervisor so that appropriate action can be taken.

Direct contact shall be avoided between the unprotected hands of personnel and raw materials, intermediate or finished, unpacked products.

8. Manufacturing Operations and Control

All manufacturing operations shall be carried out under the supervision of technical staff approved by the Licensing Authority. Each critical step in the process relating to the selection, weighing and measuring of raw material addition during various stages shall be performed by trained personnel under the direct personal supervision of approved technical staff.

Precautions against mix-up and cross-contamination

The licensee shall prevent mix-up and cross-contamination of drug material and drug product (from environmental dust) by proper air-handling system, pressure differential, segregation, status labelling and cleaning. Proper records and Standard Operating Procedures thereof shall be maintained.

The licensee shall ensure processing of sensitive drugs like Beta-Lactum antibiotics, sex hormones and cytotoxic substances in segregated are as or isolated product ion are as with in the building with independent air-handling unit and proper pressure differentials.

9. Sanitation in the Manufacturing Premises

The manufacturing premises shall be cleaned and maintained in an orderly manner, so that it is free from accumulated waste, dust, debris and other similar material. A valid cleaning procedure shall be maintained.

The manufacturing areas shall not be used for storage of materials, except for the material being processed. It shall not be used as a general thoroughfare.

A routine sanitation program shall be drawn up and observed, which shall be properly recorded and which shall indicate–

(a) Specific are as to be cleaned and cleaning intervals;

(b) Cleaning procedure to be followed, including equipment and materials to be used for cleaning; and

(c) personnel assigned to and responsible for the cleaning operation.

The adequacy of the working and in-process storage space shall permit the orderly and logical positioning of equipment and materials so as to minimize the risk of mix- up between different pharmaceutical products or their components to avoid cross contamination, and to minimise the risk of omission or wrong application of any of the manufacturing or control steps.

Production areas shall be well lit, particularly where visual on-line controls are carried out.

10. Raw Materials

(a) The licensee shall keep an inventory of all raw materials to be used at any stage of manufacture of drugs and maintain records as per Schedule U.

(b) All incoming materials shall be quarantined immediately after receipt or processing. All materials shall be stored under appropriate conditions and in an orderly fashion to permit batch segregation and stock rotation by a "first in/first expiry' first-out" principle. All incoming materials shall be checked to ensure that the consignment corresponds to the order placed.

(c) All incoming materials shall be purchased from approved sources under valid purchase vouchers. Wherever possible, raw materials should be purchased directly from the producers.

11. Equipment

(a) Equipment shall be located, designed, constructed, adapted and maintained to suit the operations to be carried out. The layout and design of the equipment shall aim to minimise the risk of errors and permit effective cleaning and maintenance in order to avoid cross-contamination, build-up of dust or dirt and, in general, any adverse effect on the quality of products. Each equipment shall be provided with a logbook, wherever necessary.

(b) Balances and other measuring equipment of an appropriate range, accuracy and precision shall be available in the raw material stores, production and in-process control operations and these shall be calibrated and checked on a scheduled basis in accordance with Standard Operating Procedures and records maintained.

(c) The parts of the production equipment that come into contact with the product shall not be reactive, additive or adsorptive to an extent that would affect the quality of the product.

12. Documentation and Records: Documentation is an essential part of the Quality assurance system and, as such, shall be related to all aspects of Good Manufacturing Practices (GMP). Its aim is to define the specifications for all materials, method of manufacture and control, to ensure that all personnel concerned with manufacture know the information necessary to decide whether or not to release a batch of a drug for sale and to provide an audit trail that shall permit investigation of the history of any suspected defective batch.

(a) Documents designed, prepared, reviewed and controlled, wherever applicable, shall comply with these rules.

(b) Documents shall be approved, signed and dated by appropriate and authorized persons.

(c) Documents shall specify the title, nature and purpose. They shall be laid out in an orderly fashion and be easy to check. Reproduced documents shall be clear and legible. Documents shall be regularly reviewed and kept up to date. Any alteration made in the entry of a document shall be signed and dated.

13. **Labels and other Printed Materials:** Labels are absolutely necessary for identification of the drugs and their use. The printing shall be done in bright colors and in a legible manner. The label shall carry all the prescribed details about the product.

14. **Quality Assurance:** This is a wide-ranging concept concerning all matters that individually or collectively influence the quality of a product. It is the totality of the arrangements made with the object of ensuring that products are of the quality required for their intended use.

15. **Self-Inspection and Quality audit:** It may be useful to constitute a self-inspection team supplemented with a quality audit procedure for assessment of all or part of a system with the specific purpose of improving it.

    Written instructions for self-inspection shall be drawn up which shall include the following:

    (a) Personnel.
    (b) Premises including personnel facilities.
    (c) Maintenance of buildings and equipment
    (d) Storage of starting materials and finished products.
    (e) Equipment.
    (f) Production and in-process controls.
    (g) Quality control.
    (h) Documentation.
    (i) Sanitation and hygiene.
    (j) Validation and revalidation programmes.
    (k) Calibration of instruments or measurements systems.
    (l) Recall procedures.

(m) Complaints management.

(n) Labels control.

(o) Results of previous self-inspections and any corrective steps take

16. Specification

For raw materials and packaging materials. They shall include-

(a) The designated name and internal code reference;

(b) reference, if any, to a pharmacopoeial monograph;

(c) qualitative and quantitative requirements with acceptance limits;

(d) name and address of manufacturer or supplier and original manufacturer of the material;

(e) specimen of printed material;

(f) directions for sampling and testing or reference to procedures;

(g) storage conditions; and

(h) maximum period of storage before re-testing.

For product containers and closures

All containers and closures intended for use shall comply with the pharmacopeial requirements. Suitable valid. test methods, sample sizes, specifications, cleaning procedure and sterilization procedure, wherever indicated, shall be strictly followed to ensure that these are not reactive, additive, absorptive, or leach to an extent that significantly affects the quality or purity of the drug. No second hand or used containers and closures shall be used.

Master Formula Records

There shall be Master Formula records relating to all manufacturing procedures for each product and batch size to be manufactured. These shall be prepared and endorsed by the competent technical staff i.e. head of production and quality control.

The Master Formula shall include:

(a) The name of the product together with product reference code relating to its specifications;

(b) the patent or proprietary name of the product along with the generic name, a description of the dosage form, strength, composition of the product and batch size;

(c) name, quantity, and reference number of all the starting materials to be used. Mention shall be made of any substance that may' disappear 'in the course of processing.

(d) a statement of the expected final yield with the acceptable limits, and of relevant intermediate yields, where applicable.

(e) A statement of the processing location and the principal equipment to be used.

(f) the methods, or reference to the methods, to be used for preparing the critical equipments including cleaning, assembling, calibrating, sterilizing;

(g) detailed stepwise processing instructions and the time taken for each step; (h) the instructions for in-process control with their limits;

(h) the requirements for storage conditions of the products, including the container, labelling and special storage conditions where applicable;

(i) any special precautions to be observed; (k) packing details and specimen labels.

Schedule N

List of minimum equipment for the efficient running of a pharmacy

1. ***Entrance:*** The front of a pharmacy shall be are an inscription —Pharmacy in front.
2. ***Premises:*** The premises of a pharmacy shall be separated from rooms for private use.
   - The premises shall be well built, dry, well-lit and ventilated and, of sufficient dimensions to allow the goods in stock, especially medicaments and poisons to be kept in a clearly visible and appropriate manner. The areas of the section to be used as dispensing department shall be not less than 6 square meters for one pharmacist working therein with additional 2 square meters for each additional pharmacist. The height of the premises shall be at least 2.5 meters.
   - The floor of the pharmacy shall be smooth and washable. The walls shall be plastered or tiled or oil painted so as to maintain smooth, durable and washable surface devoid of holes, cracks and crevices. A pharmacy shall be provided with ample supply of good quality water.
   - The dispensing department shall be separated by a barrier to prevent the admission of the public
3. ***Furniture and apparatus:*** The furniture and apparatus of a pharmacy shall be adopted to the uses for which they are intended and correspond to the size and requirements of these establishment.
   - Drugs, chemicals, and medicaments shall be kept in a room appropriate to their properties and in such special containers as will prevent any deterioration of the contents or of contents of containers

kept near them. Drawers, glasses and other containers used for keeping medicaments shall be of suitable size and capable of being closed tightly to prevent the entry of dust.

- Every container shall bear a label of appropriate size, easily readable with names of medicaments as given in the Pharmacopoeias.
- A pharmacy shall be provided with a dispensing bench, the top of which shall be covered with washable and impervious material like stainless steel, laminated or plastic, etc.
- A pharmacy shall be provided with a cupboard with lock and key for the storage of poisons and shall be clearly marked with the work 'POISON' in red letters on a white background.
- Containers of all concentrated solution shall bear special label or marked with the words —To be dilute. A Pharmacy shall be provided with the following minimum apparatus and books necessary for making of official preparations and prescriptions

Schedule P

Life Period of Drugs

Sr. No.	Name of the drug	Period between date of manu-facture and date of expiry (months)	Condition of storage
1	Ampicillin	36	In a cool place
2	Ampicillin Capsules	24	
3	Bacitracin	18	In a cool place
4	Carbenicillin Sodium Injection	24	At temperature not Exceeding 5°C
5	Colistin Sulphate	60	Protected from light
6	Gentamycin Sulphate	60	In a cool place.
7	Thiamine Mononitrate	48	In a well closed container, protected from light, in a cool place.
8	Riboflavin	60	
9	Riboflavin-5-Phosphate	24	
10	Insulin Injection	24	At temperature between 2°C and 8°C, Must not be allowed to freeze.
11	Dried Plasma	60	At a temperature not exceeding 25°C
12	Frozen Plasma	60	In deep freeze

Schedule X

[Seerule 14(1), (2), and so on]

Part 1

A. Records to be maintained

Records regarding production of ozone depleting substances

1. Dated records and related documents in respect to each producing plant, of–
   (a) The actual quantity of each ozone depleting substances produced;
   (b) The actual quantity of each ozone depleting substance used as feed stock; and
   (c) Information specified in2(b) and2(c) below. Records regarding sale and offer for sale of ozone depleting substances
2. Dated records and related documents in respect of–
   (a) The actual quantity of each ozone depleting Substances purchased
   (b) the actual quantity of each ozone depleting substances sold within India; the name and address of the recipient of each shipment and the purpose for which ozone depleting substances was purchased by the recipient. These purpose to be maintained are:
      (i) Manufacture of Aerosols
      (ii) Manufacture of foam products
      (iii) Manufacture of fire extinguishers and fire extinguishers and fire extinguishing systems.
      (iv) Manufacture of Mobile Air-conditioners
      (v) Manufacture of other Refrigeration and Air-conditioning products.
      (vi) Solvents use
      (vii) Exempted use
      (viii) Selling
      (ix) Others (please specify).

   Records regarding exports of Ozone.
3. Dated records and related documents containing information in respect of each column of Form3or4, as the case may be, of Schedule XI.

   Records regarding imports of ozone depleting substances
4. Dated records and related documents containing information in respect of each column of Form 5 or 6, as the case may be, of Schedule XI.

Record and related document of regarding manufacture import and export of compressor.

5. Dated records and related document containing information in respect of each column of form12 or13, as the case may be, of Schedule XI.

   Declaration signed by the recipient in Form12 of Schedule XI.

B. Reports to be submitted

1. Report on production of ozone depleting substances as per Form1 of Schedule XI.
2. Report on imports of ozone depleting substances as per Form 2 of Schedule XI.
3. Report on exports of ozone depleting substances as per Form 3of Schedule XI.
4. Report on sales of ozone depleting substances as per Form4 of Schedule XI.
5. Reports mentioned in Sr. No.1 to 3 above shall be submitted to the Ministry of Environment and Forests. Report mentioned in Sr. 4 above shall be submitted the registering authority specified in column (4) of Schedule V, who will submit complied version of the reports, duly countersigned will also be submitted by such authority to the Ministry of Environment& Forests in hard copy as well as in floppy on request.

Part II

A. Records to be maintained

Records regarding purchase of ozone depleting substances for use in activities specified in column (2) of Schedule IV.

1. Dated records of
   (a) the actual quantity of each ozone depleting substances purchased from an Indian supplier and the name and address of the Indian supplier;
   (b) The actual quantity of each ozone depleting substances used separately for each plant and each activity.

B. Records to be submitted

1. Report on purchase of ozone depleting substances as per Form5of Schedule XI.
2. These reports shall be submitted to the concerned registering authority specified in column (4) of Schedule V, who will submit compiled version of the report to the Ministry of Environment & Forests. Individual reports

will also be submitted by such authority to the Ministry of Environment & Forests on request.

Part III

A. Records to be maintained

Records regarding purchase of non-ozone depleting substances by beneficiary companies for use in manufacture of products.

1. Dated records and related documents in respect of:-
    1. Actual quantity of each non-ozone depleting substances purchased and then address of supplier;
    2. Actualquantityofeachnon-ozonedepletingsubstancesusedinmanufacturingoperationsseparatelyforeachplantandeachmanufacturing.

B. Reports to be submitted

1. Report on use of non-ozone depleting substances by beneficiary companies as per Form 6 of Schedule XI.
2. These reports shall be submitted to the concerned authority specified in column (4) of Schedule V, who will submit compiled version of the report to the Ministry of Environment & Forests. Individual reports will also be submitted by such authority to the Ministry of Environment & Forests on request.

Part IV

A. Records to be maintained

Records regarding reclamation

1. Dated records and related documents in respect of–
    (a) The actual quantity of each ozone depleting substances recovered ;then a mean adaddress of the individual or company from which the ozone depleting substances is recovered and the name and address, if different of the site at which the ozone depleting substances is reclaimed;
    (b) The actual quantity of each ozone depleting substances reclaimed.

B. Reports to be submitted

1. Report on reclamation of ozone depleting substances as per Form7 of Schedule XI.

2. These reports shall be submitted to the Ministry of Environment & Forests through the concerned registering authority specified in column (4) of Schedule V.

Part V

A. Records to be maintained

Records regarding destruction

1. Dated records of;

   (a) The actual quantity of each ozone depleting substances destroyed on the basis of destruction efficiency of the facility employed.

B. Reports to be submitted

1. Report on destruction of ozone depleting substances as per Form 8 of Schedule XI.
2. These reports shall be submitted to the Ministry of Environment & Forests through the concerned registering authority specified in column (4) of Schedule V.

Part VI

A. Records to be maintained

Records regarding manufacture, import and export of compressor:

1. Dated records and related documents containing information in respect of each column of Form 12 of Schedule XI.

B. Reports to be submitted

1. Report on manufacture, import, export and sale of compressor and use of refrigerants in compressors sold as per Form 12 of Schedule XI.
2. These reports shall be submitted to the concerned registering authority specified in column (4) of Schedule V, who will submit complied version of the report to the Ministry of Environment & Forests. Individual reports will also be submitted by such authority to the Ministry of Environment & Forests on request.
3. Part VII Production of records
   1. Records being maintained pursuant or requirements of rule 13 shall be available for inspection at any reasonable time on request by an officer of the registering authority specified in column (4) of Schedule V, not below in rank to a Section Officer to the Government of India,

However, persons who are engaged in selling any locally produced ozone depleting substances, except ozone depleting substances specified in Group VIII of Schedule I, shall make records available by inspection at any reasonable time on request by an officer of the concerned producing enterprise not below in rank to Assistant Manager or on request by an officer of the Ministry of Environment & Forests not below in rank to a Section Officer.

List of the Drugs which are Habit Forming and are Likely to be Misused for Addictive Purposes.

Amphetamine

Meprobamate

Phencyclidine

Barbital

Methamphetamine

Phenometrazine

Sale of Drugs

Sale of drugs: as per section 3(b) of the Drugs and Cosmetics Act,1940 drug is defined to include all the medical devices and drugs for human/animal use internally/externally for diagnosis, treatment, mitigation, treatment, and prevention of disease/disorder including preparations for repelling insects, destructing insects and also includes other components of the drug like gelatin capsules. This definition was later amended in 1964 to include Ayurvedic and Unani drugs. Sale of drugs is defined as the manufacture, cultivation, purchase, sale, or distribution of any drug, narcotic, controlled substance, or substance represented to be a drug, narcotic, or controlled substance. For the sale of drugs drug license is a prerequisite. To provide safe, effective, and quality drugs to the population, all wholesalers, manufacturers, retailers, pharmacists, dealers, and importers need to obtain drug licenses as per the Drugs and Cosmetics Act, of 1940. The license provides permission to different companies or applicants to engage in the sale of drugs as per law. In addition to obtaining a drug license the registration of establishment, and trade license are also required to sell a drug. Through licensing government maintains control over the manufacture, sale, and distribution of drugs till it is sold by retail pharmacists or wholesale pharmacists. Various types of drug licenses include Manufacturing licenses, sale licenses including wholesale licenses, retail licenses, loan licenses, import licenses, and multi-drug licenses.

Wholesale of Drugs

Wholesale is defined as an intermediate step in the marketing channel of selling products to customers without any third party included. It involves selling goods and services to those planning to resale the respective goods or services shortly. Wholesalers directly obtain goods from producers and sell these goods to retailers, industries, and other wholesalers. These buyers often buy goods in large quantities from manufacturers for further selling. Pharmaceutical wholesalers are also known as wholesale drug distributors who purchase drugs directly from manufacturers and sell them to pharmacies. The various benefits of wholesale pharmacies include lower costs, convenience, and competitive inventory. The basic requirements to obtain a wholesale license include 15 square meters business space with an air conditioner and refrigerator, a registered pharmacist with a diploma in pharmacy with one year of experience in drug dealing. Along with this online application through the website of the state licensing authority with the required fee and documents. The overall process of a wholesale license takes up to one month based on reports from drug inspector and licensing authorities and this license remains valid for 5 years and needs to be renewed on expiry. The form used to obtain a wholesale license of pharmacy as per the drugs and Cosmetics Act depends upon the category of drug to be sold. For schedule C and C (1) drugs form 21-B is used, for schedule X drugs form 20-G is used, for schedules C, C (1), and X drugs 20-B form is used. However, for Schedule C, C (1) from motor vehicles form 20-BB is used.

Retail Sale

In French, the term retailer means to break bulk. Retailing includes all activities involved in selling products and services to the ultimate consumer for their personal or home consumption. Retailers are considered the last link in the distribution channel having more knowledge about the aspirations and requirements of customers. To obtain the retail license of pharmacy, form 20-B is used for the application for sale of schedule C, C (1), excluding X form 21-B is used. Form 21-B is used for the application for the sale of Schedule C and C (1) drugs. For license of schedule X drugs form 19-C is applied. To obtain a retail license the basic requirements include minimum space of 15 square meters with AC and refrigerator, a registered pharmacist having a degree or diploma in pharmacy with one year of experience in dealing with drugs. Online application submission with said fee and documents in required form depending on the type of drug to be sold. This whole procedure may take up to 1 month depending on the drug inspector and licensing authority approval.

Documentation is a vital part of quality control which provides evidence of compliance of one process, product, and facility with GRP requirements. the documentation should follow the ALCOA and ALCOA+ principles of attributable documentation (clear identification of data along with information on who and when the process was conducted), Legible documentation (Easy understandability and readability of data by reviewer), Original documentation (Primary/original data record should be maintained), Contemporaneous document (data recorded while the activity is being performed), Accurate documentation (data recorded is error-free and reflects actual outcomes) and documentation (data compiled should be complete, enduring, consistent and available). In pharmacies records related to dispensing, prescriptions, supply, and controlled drugs need to be maintained. The duration up to which records are kept depends upon the type of document, legal requirements, and the category of drug. Some examples of records that needs to be kept in pharmacies include prescription and supply records which include electronic repeat dispensing services, patient medical records, private prescriptions, specials and unlicensed medicines, and POM register. Controlled drug records include information related to requirements, destructions, and returns of controlled drugs of different schedules. Stock handling, waste, and recall records which include stock control, first in first out, expiry dates, disposal and recall procedures of drugs. Clinical governance and patient safety records that include complaints, standard operating procedures, audits, and reporting information.

Drugs Prohibited from Manufacture and Sale in India

As per Drugs and Cosmetics Act 1940 gazette notification under section 26A following drugs have been prohibited for manufacture and sale as per the ministry of health and Family Welfare.

Some examples of prohibited drugs are: Amidopyrine, Phenacetin, Methaqualone, Nialamide, and Practolol. The complete list of drugs prohibited for sale and manufacture in India can be searched via following link.

The act also prohibits manufacturing, selling or distribution of misbranded, adulterated, spurious drugs, any patent or proprietary medicine without displaying the true formula or list of active ingredients on the container, claiming to prevent, cure and mitigate diseases which cannot be treated, harmful drugs, controversial to act provisions, drugs imported via violation of law. Manufacture of drugs without license from state licensing authority. Any violation of the set rules and laws is punished by law.

Administration of the Act and Rules

1. Advisory

a) Drug Technical Advisory Board

b) Drugs Consultative Committee

2. Analytical

a) Central Drug Laboratories

b) Drug control laboratory in states

c) Government Analysts

3. Executives

a) Licensing authorities

b) Controlling authorities

c) Drug inspectors

Drug Technical Advisory Board (DTAB)

Its advices the Central Government and the State Governments on technical matters related to the administration of this Act and at the same time carries out the other functions assigned to it by this Act. Both the nominated and elected members of the Board shall hold office for three years, but are eligible for re-nomination and re-election. The ex officio, nominated and elected members of DTAB are:

Ex-Officio

(i) Director General of Health Services (Chairman)

(ii) Drugs Controller, India

(iii) Director of the Central Drugs Laboratory, Calcutta

(iv) Director of the Central Research Institute, Kasauli

(v) Director of Indian Veterinary Research Institute, Izatnagar

(vi) President of Medical Council of India

(vii) President of the Pharmacy Council of India

(viii) Director of Central Drug Research Institute, Lucknow

Nominated

1. Two persons by the Central Government from among persons who are in charge of drugs control in the States.
2. One person by the Central Government from the pharmaceutical industry.
3. Two persons holding the appointment of Government Analyst under this Act, to be nominated by the Central Government.

Elected

1. One person, to be elected by the Executive Committee of the Pharmacy Council of India, from among teachers in pharmacy or pharmaceutical chemistry or pharmacognosy on the staff of an Indian university or a college affiliated thereto

2. One person, to be elected by the Executive Committee of the Medical Council of India, from among teachers in medicine or therapeutics on the staff of an Indian university or a college affiliated thereto;
3. One pharmacologist to be elected by the Governing Body of the Indian Council of Medical Research;
4. One person to be elected by the Central Council of the Indian Medical Association.

Drugs Consultative Committee (DCC)

It is also an advisory body constituted by central government. There are two representatives of the Central Government and One representative of each State Government. Its main function is to advice the Central Government, the State Governments and the Drugs Technical Advisory Board on any other matter tending to secure uniformity throughout India in the administration of this Act. Certain functions of DCC are:

1. Contributing Expertise: Providing specialized knowledge in pharmacology, medicine, pharmacy, toxicology, or regulatory affairs to inform decisions concerning drug-related matters.
2. Policy Development: Engaging in the creation and review of policies, guidelines, and regulations governing drug usage, safety, effectiveness, and distribution.
3. Assessment of Drug Information: Evaluating data on new drugs, including their efficacy, safety profiles, potential risks, and benefits, and making recommendations regarding approval, withdrawal, or restrictions.
4. Risk Management: Identifying potential risks associated with drug use and suggesting strategies to manage these risks and protect public health.
5. Monitoring and Surveillance: Contributing to the monitoring and surveillance efforts related to drug safety, including tracking adverse reactions, drug interactions, and emerging safety issues.
6. Clinical Trial Review: Analyzing clinical trial data submitted by pharmaceutical companies to assess the effectiveness and safety of experimental drugs.
7. Public Education: Participating in educational campaigns targeting healthcare professionals, patients, and the general public to promote safe and responsible drug use.
8. Collaboration and Communication: Working with healthcare professionals, regulatory bodies, industry representatives, and other stakeholders to share information, discuss best practices, and address challenges in the realm of drug management.

9. Ethical Considerations: Ensuring that discussions and decisions related to drug regulation and usage uphold ethical principles and prioritize public health and safety.

Central Drug Laboratory (CDL)

There are seven central drug testing laboratories under CDSCO. These are at Kolkata, Mumbai, Chennai, Guwahati, Chandigarh, Kasuali and Hyderabad. The various functions exhibited by CDL are:

- Drug Analysis: The CDL conducts thorough analysis of pharmaceuticals, both finished products and raw materials, to ensure they meet established standards for safety, efficacy, and quality.
- Quality Control: It establishes and upholds quality control measures to verify the consistency and reliability of drug products in circulation, thereby protecting public health.
- Reference Standards: Maintaining a repository of reference standards for drugs and pharmaceutical substances, which serve as benchmarks for quality assessment and comparison during testing.
- Research and Development: Engaging in research endeavors aimed at advancing analytical techniques, refining testing methodologies, and addressing emerging challenges in drug quality and safety.
- Regulatory Assistance: The CDL offers technical expertise and aid to regulatory bodies in formulating and enforcing drug regulations, standards, and policies.
- Capacity Enhancement: Offering training initiatives, workshops, and seminars to enhance the capabilities and knowledge of professionals involved in drug testing, quality control, and regulatory affairs.
- Collaborative Efforts: Collaborating with national and international entities, regulatory authorities, research institutions, and industry stakeholders to exchange insights, disseminate best practices, and tackle common issues in drug testing and regulation.
- Emergency Response: In situations of drug-related emergencies, like suspected adulteration or contamination, the CDL may play a pivotal role in swiftly conducting testing and analysis to evaluate risks and facilitate appropriate regulatory measures

Licensing Authorities

Government Analyst

Both the state government and central government are responsible for appointing the government analyst. A notification is released in official gazette for the appointment of an individual as government analyst only if person fulfills the given criteria of qualification. The central and state government both appoints the Government analyst in the desired areas of certain state.

(a) The basic qualification criteria for government analyst are a graduate either in field of medicine/science/pharmacy or in pharmaceutical chemistry form a recognized university. Along with the graduation a five-year experience is mandatory especially in testing of drugs in laboratory that too under the guidance of head of approved institution.

(b) Similarly, an individual with post-graduation in medicine/science/pharmacy or in pharmaceutical chemistry is applicable for the post of government analyst. He should also possess a 3-year experience in testing of drugs in laboratory under the control of head of approved institution.

A large range of duties are to be performed by Government Analysts like analysis of sample of drugs or cosmetics as sent to him either by the inspectors or by private organizations and at the same time to prepare the reports accordingly. Also to provide a regular update to the government about the reports dealing with the results of the sample and other necessary information about the sample.

Drug Inspectors

Drug inspectors recognized as the public servants are appointed both by the state and central government. To become a drug inspector an individual should not hold any profit of organization that is he shall be free from any financial gains related to sale, manufacture, export or import of drugs or cosmetic. The necessary qualifications to become drug inspector are discussed below:

(a) An individual shall possess a graduation in medicine with specialization in Clinical pharmacology, Microbiology, pharmacy or in pharmaceutical chemistry from a recognized university.

(b) For inspection of manufacture of substances in schedule C, at least 18 month experience in manufacturing and testing of at least one of the substances specified in schedule C is mandatory.

The government has vested large number of powers to drug inspector like inspection, collection of samples, and examine data.

- Drug inspector can inspect anytime all such premises that deal with manufacturing, distribution and sale the drugs or cosmetics.
- Any drug or cosmetic which is being manufactured sold or distributed can be collected anytime as sample to evaluate whether it meets the basic quality and efficacy parameters.

- Drug inspector may examine the records of distribution and manufacturing of drugs and could seize the batch if it is unfit or adulterated.
- Drug inspector enquires about the complaints related to drug a raised either by the customers, or by healthcare.
- Implement suitable measures to enforce regulations like by imposing fine or by suspending certain operation for a specific time period and could initiate drug recall process.

CHAPTER 4

Narcotic Drugs and Psychotropic Substances Act 1985 and Rules

Introduction

The Narcotic Drugs and Psychotropic Substances Act, 1985, stands as a sentinel against the growing challenges posed by the illicit trade, abuse, and trafficking of narcotic drugs and psychotropic substances in India. Enacted against the backdrop of a burgeoning global concern surrounding narcotics, this legislation serves as the nation's legal bulwark, meticulously crafted to strike a balance between ensuring the availability of controlled substances for legitimate medical and scientific purposes and staunchly preventing their misuse. In response to international conventions and a heightened recognition of the need for a robust regulatory framework, the Indian government promulgated this landmark legislation. The Act not only reflects a commitment to national and international obligations but also addresses the dynamic landscape of substance abuse, acknowledging the multifaceted dimensions of the issue. This legal framework provides a comprehensive approach, encompassing the definition of substances, delineation of authorities and officers responsible for enforcement, establishment of stringent controls, and imposition of penalties for offenses. Rooted in the principles of prevention, control, and cooperation, the Act signifies the nation's resolve to fight the global menace of narcotics, encouraging a healthier and safer society. As we search into the intricacies of the Narcotic Drugs and Psychotropic Substances Act, 1985, it becomes evident that the legislation not only embodies the spirit of safeguarding public welfare but also exemplifies India's commitment to international collaboration in the global fight against drug-related challenges. This introduction sets the stage for a closer examination of the Act's provisions, objectives, and the multifaceted strategies it employs to navigate the complex terrain of narcotics regulation.

Objectives

The objectives of The Narcotic Drugs and Psychotropic Substances Act, 1985, and its accompanying rules are comprehensive and progressive, reflecting the multifaceted nature of the challenges posed by narcotic drugs and psychotropic substances. The primary goals of the Act can be categorized as follows:

1. **Prevention of Illicit Trafficking:** A core objective of the Act is the proactive prevention and combat of illicit trafficking in narcotic drugs and psychotropic substances. Illicit trafficking not only contributes to the proliferation of substance abuse but also poses a threat to public health and safety. The Act, through its firm measures, aims to restrict and eliminate the unlawful trade of these substances, recognizing the grave consequences of unregulated trafficking on society. By imposing strict penalties and creating a robust regulatory framework, the Act attempts to discourage individuals and organizations involved in the illicit trade of narcotic drugs and psychotropic substances.
2. **Control and Regulation:** The Act seeks to establish effective control and regulation over various operations related to narcotic drugs and psychotropic substances. This objective is two-fold, first, to ensure that these substances are available for legitimate medical and scientific purposes, and second, to prevent their misuse and diversion for illicit purposes. By implementing licensing and permit systems, the Act empowers regulatory authorities to monitor and control the production, distribution, and use of these substances. This not only safeguards public health but also contributes to maintaining a delicate balance between availability and restriction.
3. **International Cooperation:** Recognizing the transnational nature of the narcotics trade, the Act places a strong emphasis on international cooperation. By collaborating with other nations, India aims to enforce effective control measures and adhere to international conventions governing the regulation of narcotic drugs and psychotropic substances. This objective underscores the affiliations of global efforts to fight against drug-related challenges. Through information sharing, joint operations, and mutual assistance, the Act encourages a coordinated approach to tackling the complex and ever-evolving issue of narcotics trafficking. International cooperation not only strengthens the enforcement mechanisms but also contributes to a unified front against the global drug menace.

Definition

Narcotic Drugs: The term "Narcotic Drugs" under the Act pertains to substances enumerated in Schedules I and II. These schedules comprehensively list substances deemed as narcotic drugs, including but not limited to opium, heroin, cannabis, and other substances with similar psychoactive properties. By categorizing these substances, the Act provides a definitive list, facilitating the identification and regulation of narcotics based on their inherent properties and potential for abuse.

Psychotropic Substances: "Psychotropic Substances" are substances outlined in Schedules III and IV of the Act. These schedules encompass a range of substances, including hallucinogens and amphetamines, known for their impact on the central nervous system and potential psychoactive effects. By specifying the substances falling under this category, the Act ensures a comprehensive understanding of psychotropic substances, aiding in their control, regulation, and prevention of misuse.

Manufacture: The term "Manufacture" is defined in the Act to encompass various activities related to the production, cultivation, extraction, preparation, possession, sale, purchase, transport, warehousing, use, consumption, import, inter-state export, inter-state import into India, export from India, or trans-shipment of narcotic drugs and psychotropic substances. This broad definition encompasses the entire spectrum of activities involved in the life cycle of these substances, ensuring that all aspects of their production and distribution are subject to regulatory control.

Authorities and Officer

The Narcotic Drugs and Psychotropic Substances Act, 1985, outlines a structured framework of authorities and officers tasked with enforcing and implementing the provisions of the Act. These key entities play crucial roles in the control, regulation, and enforcement of operations related to narcotic drugs and psychotropic substances:

1. **Central Government:** The Central Government is entrusted with substantial powers under the Act, empowering it to take measures for the effective control and regulation of operations related to narcotic drugs and psychotropic substances. This ambient authority ensures that the highest levels of governance are involved in formulating policies, coordinating efforts, and adapting strategies to address the evolving challenges posed by the illicit trade and abuse of controlled substances.
2. **Narcotics Control Bureau (NCB):** The Narcotics Control Bureau serves as a specialized agency established to coordinate and execute actions among various authorities for the thorough implementation of the provisions of the Act. The NCB plays a crucial role in intelligence gathering, investigation, and collaboration with other law enforcement agencies to fight against illicit trafficking and restrict the misuse of narcotic drugs and psychotropic substances. Through its specialized focus, the NCB contributes to the overall effectiveness of the regulatory framework envisioned by the Act.

3. **Designated Officers:** The Act designates specific individuals as "Designated Officers" who are entrusted with the authority to investigate and enforce the provisions of the Narcotic Drugs and Psychotropic Substances Act, 1985. These officers operate at various levels of law enforcement and are responsible for executing the regulatory measures outlined in the Act. Designated Officers are essential in ensuring that the regulatory framework is implemented on the ground, conducting investigations, making arrests, and taking legal actions against those violating the provisions of the Act.

   Together, these key authorities and officers form a cohesive network aimed at achieving the objectives of the Act. The Central Government provides ambient guidance and policy direction, the Narcotics Control Bureau serves as a specialized coordinating agency, and Designated Officers operate at the frontline, actively enforcing the regulatory measures to prevent illicit trafficking and misuse of narcotic drugs and psychotropic substances. This collaborative and hierarchical structure is integral to the effective functioning of the regulatory framework envisioned by the legislation.

Prohibition, Control and Regulation

Prohibition

The Act explicitly prohibits a wide range of activities associated with narcotic drugs and psychotropic substances, except when authorized for medical and scientific purposes. This prohibition encompasses activities such as production, cultivation, manufacture, possession, sale, purchase, transportation, warehousing, consumption, import, export, and transshipment of these substances. The stringent prohibition measures are aimed at curbing illicit trafficking and preventing the misuse of controlled substances, thereby safeguarding public health and welfare. However, the Act also provides exemptions for certain activities undertaken for legitimate medical and scientific purposes, subject to compliance with specified regulations and procedures.

Control and Regulation

The Central Government is vested with the authority to regulate and control various facets related to narcotic drugs and psychotropic substances. This includes the issuance of licenses, permits, and authorizations for activities such as cultivation, production, manufacture, storage, distribution, sale, transportation, and use of these substances. By exercising control over these aspects, the Central Government ensures a balanced approach to availability and restriction, thereby preventing misuse while facilitating access for legitimate purposes. Additionally, the Act empowers regulatory authorities to monitor and enforce compliance with prescribed regulations, conduct inspections, and take necessary measures to prevent diversion and misuse of controlled substances.

Offenses and Penalties

The NDPS Act, 1985 lays out strict rules and penalties to discourage people from breaking the law:

Punishment for Contravention: If someone goes against the rules of the Act, they can face serious consequences. This includes imprisonment, which means they might have to go to jail, and fines, where they have to pay a sum of money as a penalty for their actions. These penalties are meant to deter people from breaking the law and engaging in activities related to narcotic drugs and psychotropic substances.

Enhanced Punishment: For those who repeatedly break the law or are involved in serious offenses involving large amounts of drugs, the punishments are even harsher. This means they might face longer prison sentences or higher fines to reflect the seriousness of their actions. Repeat offenders and those involved in large-scale illegal activities face heightened penalties to discourage them from continuing their illegal activities.

Forfeiture of Property: The Act also allows for the confiscation or forfeiture of property that is obtained from or used in the commission of specific offenses. This means that if someone has gained property through illegal activities related to drugs, such as selling them, the government can take away that property as a punishment.

Abetment and Criminal Conspiracy: The Act addresses situations where people encourage or help others to break the law, known as abetment, and situations where people plan together to commit crimes, known as criminal conspiracy. Those involved in such activities can also face punishment under the Act, ensuring that everyone involved in illegal activities related to narcotic drugs and psychotropic substances is held accountable.

CHAPTER 5

Drug and Magic Remedies (Objectionable Advertisement) Act 1954

Definition

The Act regulates drug advertisement, prohibits the promotion of remedies claiming magical properties, and addresses related matters including a talisman, mantra, kavacha, and any other charm of any kind that is alleged to possess miraculous power. It aims to protect consumers from misleading advertising of drugs and remedies with unproven magical properties, and establishes guidelines for transparent and accurate pharmaceutical product advertising practices.

Objectives

Preventing Misleading Advertisements: One of the primary objectives of the Act is to prevent the dissemination of misleading or false advertisements related to drugs and remedies. Such advertisements often make exaggerated claims about the efficacy of certain drugs or remedies, which can mislead consumers and endanger their health.

1. **Protecting Public Health:** By regulating the advertisement of drugs and remedies, the Act aims to protect public health. It seeks to ensure that only those drugs and remedies that have been scientifically proven to be safe and effective are promoted to the public.
2. **Curbing Quackery:** The Act aims to curb quackery by prohibiting advertisements that claim to possess magic qualities for the treatment of diseases. Quackery refers to the practice of promoting unproven or fraudulent medical treatments, which can be harmful to individuals seeking effective healthcare.
3. **Promoting Rational Drug Use:** By regulating drug advertisements, the Act contributes to promoting rational drug use. It discourages the unnecessary consumption of drugs and remedies based on false or exaggerated claims, thereby encouraging individuals to seek appropriate medical advice and treatment.

4. **Regulating the Pharmaceutical Industry:** The Act forms part of the regulatory framework governing the pharmaceutical industry in India. It helps ensure compliance with ethical standards and prevents the exploitation of consumers through deceptive advertising practices.

Commencement

It extends to the whole of India except the State of Jammu and Kashmir in 1954, amd applies also to persons domiciled in the territories to which this act extend who are outside the said territories.

Prohibition of Certain Advertisement

Indian law enacted to regulate the advertising of drugs and remedies that claim to have magical or miraculous properties. The Act aims to prevent misleading advertisements that could lead to the consumption of ineffective or harmful substances by the public.

- ✓ Under the Drug and Magic Remedies Act 1985, it is illegal to advertise any drug or remedy that:
  1. Makes a claim to cure or mitigate diseases considered incurable or serious in nature.
  2. Claims to confer magical powers or properties in curing ailments.
  3. Suggests that the drug or remedy is guaranteed or entirely safe without proper scientific evidence.
  4. Contains any matter that directly or indirectly gives a false impression regarding the true character of the drug or remedy.

Classes of Prohibited Advertisement

Under the Drug and Magic Remedies Act 1985, certain advertisements may be exempted from the prohibition if they fall into specific categories. These exemptions are typically designed to allow for the dissemination of accurate and beneficial information while still maintaining safeguards against deceptive marketing practices. For example, advertisements for certain types of vitamins, minerals, and other dietary supplements may be exempt from the prohibition if they meet specific criteria outlined in the Act. This helps ensure that consumers have access to important information about these products while also protecting them from false or misleading claims.

- ✓ Some exempted advertisements may include:
  - (a) **Prescription Medications:** Advertisements directed exclusively to licensed healthcare professionals for prescription drugs may be exempted. These advertisements often provide important

information for healthcare professionals to make informed decisions about prescribing medications to patients.

(b) **Educational Material:** Advertisements that provide purely educational or informational content about diseases, treatments, or health-related topics may be exempted. These advertisements aim to raise awareness and promote public health without making specific claims about the efficacy or availability of particular drugs or remedies.

(c) **Scientific Journals and Publications:** Advertisements published in scientific journals or other reputable publications that are intended for healthcare professionals may be exempted. These advertisements often contain peer-reviewed research and data about drugs, treatments, or medical devices.

(d) **Governmental Health Campaigns:** Advertisements sponsored or endorsed by government health agencies as part of public health campaigns may be exempted. These campaigns typically aim to raise awareness about specific health issues, promote healthy behaviours, or provide information about available healthcare services.

(e) **Product Labelling and Packaging:** Advertisements that are limited to labeling or packaging of drugs or remedies and comply with regulatory requirements may be exempted. These advertisements typically provide essential information about dosage, administration, side effects, and contraindications for consumers.

(f) **Healthcare Services:** Advertisements for healthcare services, such as hospitals, clinics, or medical professionals, may be exempted. These advertisements often focus on promoting the availability of healthcare services and may include general information about the types of treatments or procedures offered.

Classes of Prohibited Advertisement Includes

Section 01: Prohibition of Advertisement of Certain Drugs for Treatment of certain Diseases and Disorders

- The procurement of miscarriage in women or prevention of conception in women; or
- The maintenance or improvement of the capacity of human beings for sexual pleasure;
- The correction of menstrual disorder in women; or

- The diagnosis, cure, mitigation, treatment or prevention of any disease, disorder or condition specified in the Schedule, or any other disease, disorder or condition which may be specified in the rules made under this Act (**Schedule J**).

Names of the Diseases, Disorder and Conditions as per Schedule

- Appendicitis. 2.
- Arteriosclerosis
- Blindness
- Blood poisoning
- Bright's disease
- Cancer
- Deafness
- Cataract
- Diabetes
- Diseases and disorders of the brain
- Diseases and disorders of the optical system
- Diseases and disorders of the uterus
- Disorders of the menstrual flow
- Disorders of the nervous system
- Disorders of the prostatic gland
- Dropsy
- Epilepsy
- Female disease (in general)
- Fevers (in general)
- Fits
- Forms and structure of the female bust
- Gallstones, kidney stones and bladder stones
- Gangrene
- Glaucoma
- Goiter
- Heart diseases
- High or low blood pressure
- Hydrocele
- Hysteria

- Infantile paralysis
- Insanity
- Leprosy
- Leukoderma
- Lockjaw
- Locomotor ataxia
- Lupus
- Nervous debility
- Obesity
- Paralysis
- Plague
- Pleurisy
- Pneumonia
- Rheumatism
- Ruptures
- Sexual impotence
- Smallpox
- Stature of persons
- Sterility in women
- Trachoma
- Tuberculosis
- Tumors
- Typhoid fever
- Ulcers of GIT
- Venereal disease, including syphilis, gonorrhoea, soft chancre, venereal granuloma and lympho granuloma

Section 02: Prohibition of Misleading Advertisements Relating to Drugs

Subject to the provisions of this Act, no person shall take any part in the publication of any advertisement relating to a drug if the advertisement contains any matter which-

- Directly or indirectly gives false impression regarding the true nature or character of the drug, or

- Makes a false claim for the drug; or
- Is otherwise false or misleading in any material particular are prohibited.

Section 03: Prohibition of Advertisement of Magic Remedies for Treatment of Certain Diseases and Disorders

No person carrying on or purporting to carry on the profession of administering magic remedies shall take any part in the publication of any advertisement referring to any magic remedy that directly or indirectly claims to be efficacious for any of the purposes specified in **Section 3**.

1. **Prohibition of Import into, and export from, India of certain Advertisements:**

   No person shall import into, or export from, the territories to which this Act extends any documents containing an advertisement of the nature referred to in Section 3 or in Section 4 or Section 5, and any document containing any such advertisements shall be deemed to be goods of which the import or export has been prohibited under section 19 of the Sea Customs Act, 1878 (8 of 1878), and all the provisions of that act shall have effect accordingly.

Offences and Penalties

Penalty: whoever contravenes any of the provisions of this Act of the rules made there under shall, on conviction, ne punishable-

(a) In the case of **first conviction**, with imprisonment which may extend to six months, or with a fine, or with both;

(b) In the case of a subsequent conviction, with imprisonment which may extend to one year, or with a fine, or with both.

Offences by Companies

1. If the person contravening any of the provisions of this Act is a company, every person who, at the time the offences were committed, was in charge of and was responsible to the company for the conduct of the business of the company as well as the company shall be deemed to be guilty of the contravention and shall be liable to the proceeded against punished accordingly;

   Provided that nothing contained in this sub section shall render any such person liable to any punishment provided in this Act if he proves that the offence was committed without his knowledge or that he exercised all due diligence to prevent the commission of such offence.

2. Notwithstanding anything contained in sub section (10 where an) offence under this Act has been committed by a company and it is proved that the

offence was committed with the consent or connivance of or is attributable to any neglect on the part of any director manager secretary or other officer of the company shall also be deemed to be guilty of that offence and shall be liable to be proceeded against any punished accordingly.

CHAPTER 6

Prevention of Cruelty to Animals Act-1960

Introduction

The Prevention of Cruelty to Animals Act, 1960 is legislation enacted in India to prevent the infliction of unnecessary pain or suffering on animals and to promote their welfare. The act provides guidelines for the treatment and care of animals, including provisions for their housing, feeding, and medical needs. It also prohibits certain cruel practices such as animal fighting, mutilation, and abandonment. Additionally, the act establishes penalties for those found guilty of animal cruelty, aiming to ensure that animals are treated with compassion and respect throughout the country.

The Act extends to the whole of India, except for the State of Jammu and Kashmir, and came into force on April 1, 1961. The Act has several provisions, including the establishment of the Animal Welfare Board of India, duties of persons having charge of animals, regulation of performing animals, and penalties for committing offenses under the Act. The Act has been amended several times, with the most recent amendment being the Animal Welfare (Amendment) Act, 2019. The Act is enforced by the Animal Welfare Board of India, which is responsible for ensuring the welfare of animals and preventing cruelty.

The Animal Welfare Board of India plays a crucial role in implementing and enforcing the provisions of the Act. It conducts inspections, investigates complaints, and takes necessary actions to ensure the well-being of animals and punish those who commit offenses against them. Additionally, the Act also encourages public participation in animal welfare activities and promotes awareness about animal rights and protection.

Objectives

- To prevent the infliction of unnecessary pain or suffering on animals as well as to prevent cruelty to animals.
- To provide for punishment for causing unnecessary cruelty and suffering to animals. The Act defines animals and different forms of animals.

- The term animals comprise of any living creature but not the human being.
- To provide the guidelines relating to experimentation on animals for scientific purposes.

CPCSEA

The CPCSEA, or the Committee for the Purpose of Control and Supervision of Experiments on Animals, is an organization in India that oversees and regulates the use of animals in scientific research and experimentation. Established under the Prevention of Cruelty to Animals Act, 1960, the CPCSEA works to ensure that experiments involving animals are conducted with ethical considerations and that the well-being of animals is safeguarded.

The motto of the Prevention to Animals (PCA) Act 1960 as amended in 1982, is to prevent infliction of unnecessary pain or suffering on animals. The Central Government has constituted a CPCSEA which is duty bound to take all such measures as may be necessary to ensure that animals are not subjected to unnecessary pain or suffering before, during or after the performance of experiments on them. For this purpose, the government has made the "Breeding of and Experiments on Animals (Control and Supervision) Rules, 1998" as amended during 2001 and 2006, to regulate the experimentation on animals.

Rules made by the Committee

1. In cases where experiments are performed in any institution, the responsibility therefore is placed on the person in charge of the institution and that, in cases where experiments are performed outside an institution by individuals, the individuals are qualified on that behalf and the experiments are performed under their supervision.
2. Experiments are performed with due care and humanity, and that as far as possible experiments involving operations are performed under the influence of some anaesthetic of sufficient power to prevent the animals from feeling pain.
3. That animal which, in the course of experiments under the influence of anesthetics, are so injured that their recovery would involve serious suffering, are ordinarily destroyed while still insensible.
4. Experiments on animals are avoided wherever it is possible to do so; as for example, in medical schools, hospitals, colleges and the like, if other teaching devices such as books, models, films and the like may equally suffice.

5. Experiments on larger animals are avoided when it is possible to achieve the same results by experiments upon small laboratory animals like guinea-pigs, rabbits, frogs and rats.
6. As far as possible, experiments are not performed merely for the purpose of acquiring manual skill.
7. Suitable records are maintained with respect to experiments performed on animals.

Function's

- Registration of establishments conducting animal experimentation or breeding of animals for this purpose.
- Selection and appointment of nominees in the Institutional Animals Ethics Committees of registered establishment.
- Approval of Animal house Facilities on the basis of reports of inspections conducted by CPCSEA.
- Permission for conducting experiments involving use of animals.
- Recommendation for imports of animals for use in experiments.
- Action against establishments in case of violation of any legal norm/stipulation.

Goals

1. The goal of these guidelines is to promote the human care of animal used in biomedical and behavioral research and testing.
2. To avoid unnecessary pain before, and after the experiment.
3. To provide guideline for –
    - Housing, care, breeding and maintenance
    - Source of experimental animals.
    - Acceptable experimental procedures for anesthesia and euthanasia.
4. To regulate experimentation on the animal, the committee has formulated "Breeding of and experiments on animals (control and supervision) rules, 1998" which were amended in 2001 and then in 2006.

Institutional Animal Ethics Committee

A body comprising of a group of persons recognized and registered by the CPCSEA performed in an establishment which is constituted and operated in accordance with procedures specified for the purpose by the Committee;

- The primary duty of IAEC is to work for the achievement of the objectives.
- IAEC will review and approve all types of research proposals involving small animal experimentation before the start of the study. For

experimentation on large animals, the case is required to be forwarded to CPCSEA in prescribed manner with the recommendation of IAEC.

- IAEC is required to monitor the research throughout the study and after completion of study through periodic reports and visit to animal house and laboratory where the experiments are conducted. The committee has to ensure compliance with all regulatory requirements, applicable rules, guidelines and laws.

Composition of IAEC

- An IAEC typically includes:
  - A Biological Scientist.
  - Two Scientists from different biological disciplines.
  - A Veterinarian involved in animal care.
  - The Scientist In-Charge of the Animal House Facility.
  - The Chairman (preferably Head of the Institution/Department) and Member Secretary nominated by CPCSEA.
  - Other members, including Main Nominee, Link Nominee, Scientist from outside, and Socially Aware Nominee.

Breeding and Stocking of Animals

For initiating a colony, the breeding stock must be procured from CPCSEA registered breeders or suppliers ensuring that genetic makeup and health status of animal is known. In case of an inbred strain, the characters of the strain with their gene distribution and the number of inbreed generations must be known for further propagation. The health status should indicate their origin, for example conventional, specific pathogen free or transgenic, gnotobiotic or knockout stock. Only the registered establishments can carry out the business of breeding or trading animals for performing experiments on them.

The breeder or the establishment carrying on this business should apply for registration within 60 days from the date of starting the Breeding of and Experiments on Animals (Control and Supervision) Rules, 1998 (CPCSEA). In case the Committee denies giving registration, the breeder should stop animal breeding. The breeder or the establishment should apply for registration (in the prescribed format), either to the Member-Secretary or any other person appointed by the Committee on this behalf. The breeder or the establishment should stock the animals as specified. Animal houses should be located in a quiet atmosphere with no traffic. The buildings should be neat, hygienic, and the animals should be protected from drought and extreme conditions of weather. Small animals should be kept in cages and large animals should be given shelter under stables for their comfort and to avoid overcrowding.

The animals should also be looked after during off hours and on holidays. The cages or the racks for the animals should follow the standards given by the Indian Standards Institution (ISI). The attendants of the animals should be well- trained and experienced in their work. The Committee or IAEC should lay down some conditions to make sure that the animals do not suffer from needless pain or problems either before, during, or after the experiments have been performed on them. These conditions become effective when the Committee plans to approve the conduction of experiments. The Committee can also ask for information or reports after the experiments from the establishments, IAEC, and individuals performing experiments on animals.

Performance of Experiments

As per the rules of this Act, no illegal experiments or experiments on animals for discovering physiological knowledge or knowledge valuable in saving or lengthening life or decreasing suffering or fighting any disease (in human beings, animals, or plants) should be performed. When the Central Government after being advised by the Board holds view at it is required to regulate or supervise the experiments on animals, the Official Gazette should constitute a committee comprising of sufficient number of officials as well as non-officials. The Chairman of the Committee should be appointed by the Central Government. This Committee should have the power to regulate its own procedure in order to perform its duties effectively. The funds of the Committee should contain grants (often made to it by the Government) and contributions, donations, subscriptions, bequests, gifts, etc. (made to it by any other person).

In particular and without any prejudice to the generalization of the earlier power, rules made by the Committee should secure the following objects:

1. When experiments are performed in any institution, the responsibility is placed on its in-charge; and when experiments are performed by individuals outside an institution, the individuals are held responsible for the experiments.
2. The experiments are performed carefully and kindly under the effect of anesthesia so that the animals do not sense the pain.
3. The animals injured during the experiments and those who would suffer severely:
4. The experiments on animals in medical schools, hospitals, colleges, etc. (should be avoided if sufficient books, models, films, etc. teaching devices are available.
5. Performing experiments on large animals if sufficient results can be attained should be avoided by conducting experiments on small laboratory animals (such as guinea-pigs, rabbits, frogs, and rats).

6. The experiments should not be performed merely to gain manual skill.
7. The animals on which experiments are to be performed should be carefully looked after before and even after the experiments.
8. Records should be maintained with respect to the experiments performed on animals.

The inspection report madc by an officer (appointed by the Committee) is thoroughly checked by the Committee. If the Committee remains dissatisfied and feels that the rules made by it are not being followed, it can refuse to give permission to the person or institution to further conduct experiments (after warning the person or institution).

This ban is either for a limited time period or permanent; however, the person or the institution can conduct experiments on certain situations imposed by the Committee.

Transfer and Acquisition of Animals for Experiment

Transport of animals from one place to another is very important and must be undertaken with care. The main considerations for transport of animals are, mode of transport, containers, animal density in cages, food and water during transit, protection from transit infections, injuries and stress.

The mode of transport of animals depends on the distance, seasonal and climatic conditions and the species of animals. Animals can be transported by road, rail or air taking into consideration of above factors.

In any case the transport stress should be avoided and the containers should be of an appropriate size so as to enable these animals to have a comfortable, free movement and protection from possible injuries.

The food and water should be provided in suitable containers or in suitable form so as to ensure that they get adequate food and more particularly water during transit. The transport containers (cages or crates) should be of appropriate size and 38 only a permissible number of animals should be accommodated in each container to avoid overcrowding and infighting.

The guidelines put forward by the Committee for controlling and suspending experiments on animals should be obeyed by the breeder or the establishment. Importing an animal which is already available in the country by a breeder or establishment is also not legalized.

Records

1. The Animal House should maintain following records :
    - Animal House plans, which includes typical floor plan, all fixtures etc.

- Animal House staff record - both technical and non-technical.
- Health record of staff.
- All SOPs relevant to the animals.
- Breeding, stock, purchase and sales records.
- Minutes of institute Animals Ethics Committee Meetings.
- Records of experiments conducted with the number of animals used.
- Death Record.
- Clinical record of sick animals.
- Training record of staff involved.

Standard Operating Procedure

The Standard Operating Procedures (SOPs) as per the Committee for the Purpose of Control and Supervision of Experiments on Animals (CPCSEA) cover various aspects of the ethical and humane use of animals in experiments. Some of the SOPs available include:

- ➢ Maintain standard operating procedure (SOP) describing procedures/ methods adapted with regard to animal husbandry, maintenance, breeding, animal house microbial analysis and experimentation record.
- ➢ SOP should contain following items: -
    - Name of author
        - Title of SOP
        - Date of preparation
        - Reference of previous SOP on the same subject and date
    - Location and distribution of SOPs with sign of each recipient
    - Objectives
    - Detailed information of the instruments used in relation with animals
    - Normal value of all parameters.

A record (in the prescribed format) of the animals under the control and custody of every establishment or IAEC should be maintained and presented to the Committee whenever asked for. The number or species of animal's possessed by the laboratories should be informed (in the prescribed format) to the Secretary or any other officer appointed by the Committee on this behalf.

Power to Suspend or Revoke Registration

If an establishment or breeder violates any laws pertaining to the morally and humanely acceptable use of animals in research, the CPCSEA has the authority to suspend or cancel their registration. If there is a significant infraction, CPCSEA has the authority to issue formal orders suspending or revoking the establishment's registration and/or ordering the animal house facility to close. The authority to revoke or suspend registration is a crucial tool for ensuring that organizations follow the laws and policies pertaining to the moral and humanly use of animals in research. Establishments and breeders are discouraged by this approach from prioritizing the well-being of animals during trials. It also emphasizes the significance of ethical and humane practices in scientific research, promoting a culture of responsible animal use in the field.

When the rules put forward by the Committee are not obeyed by any establishment, breeder, or IAEC, it may cancel their registration after giving a warning either for a definite time period or permanently. The Committee can permit the establishment, breeder, or IAEC to continue to work according to certain conditions enforced by the Committee.

The Committee can cancel the registration of any establishment or breeder not acting in accordance with the provisions. The Committee can make some guidelines for caring and protecting animals which are under the custody of any establishment or breeder, whose registration is being cancelled. These guidelines should be immediately considered by the establishment or breeder so that they are not prohibited from performing experiments on animals, or from obtaining or transferring animals.

Offences and Penalties

- An individual is held responsible of an offence under this Act, if he/she:
  1. Exhibits or trains any animal not registered under this amendment,
  2. Exhibits or trains any animal with respect to which he/she is not registered,
  3. Exhibits or trains any animal on which experiments should not be conducted,
- An individual is held responsible of an offence under this Act, if he/she:
  4. Does not allow any individual or police officer to enter and inspect the place where experiments are conducted,
  5. Hides any animal to avoid inspection,
  6. Despite being registered under this Act, fails to produce the certificate with no genuine reason.
  7. Applies to get registered under this Act when not entitled to be so registered.

If found to be guilty of any of these offences, an individual is punished with a fine of 500 or is imprisoned for 3 months or both.

On contravening any condition enforced by the Committee, an individual is punished with a fine up to 200. If the contravention of rules takes place in any institution, the in-charge of it should is held responsible for the offence and punished.

CHAPTER 7

Poison Act-1919

Introduction

The Poison Act, 1919, was enacted on 3rd September, 1919, to regulate the importation, possession, and sale of poisons in India. The Act of 1919 replaced the poison Act of 1904. The Act empowers the central government to regulate the import of poisons, while various state governments are authorized to make rules regarding the possession and sale of poisons within their respective states.

In addition to these regulations, as per the Poison Act of 1919, it is also required that individuals selling or distributing poisonous substances should obtain a license. This license ensured that those handling these substances were knowledgeable about their potential dangers and could safely handle them. Furthermore, the act mandated that all the licensed individuals keep records of their sales and distributions, providing a means for authorities to track the movement of these substances and investigate any suspicious or illegal activities. By implementing these measures, the Poison Act of 1919 aimed to create a system of accountability and oversight within the industry, ultimately safeguarding the public from the potential harm posed by these dangerous substances.

For example, under the Poison Act of 1919, pharmacies and chemical manufacturers were required to train their employees on the proper handling and storage of toxic substances such as arsenic or mercury. This ensured that only knowledgeable individuals could handle these substances, reducing the risk of accidents or intentional misuse. Additionally, the act mandated that pharmacies maintain detailed records of their sales and distributions, allowing authorities to identify any patterns of suspicious activity or illegal trafficking of poisonous substances. This enabled law enforcement agencies to investigate and prevent potential.

The Act covers various aspects such as:

1. Safe custody of poisons
2. Labeling of vessels, packages, or coverings in which poisons are sold or possessed for sale
3. Issuance of search warrants
4. Penalties for unlawful importation, possession, or sale of poisons

Scope

The scope of the act includes the entire country, with the exception of the state of Jammu and Kashmir, except to the extent to which the provisions of this Act relate to the importation into India of any specified poison.

The Poison Act of 1919 in India primarily focuses on regulating and controlling the importation of specified poisons across customs frontiers. The key provisions of the Act empower the Central Government to prohibit the import of designated poisons, unless done under and in accordance with the conditions specified in a license. The Act grants the Central Government, the authority to define customs frontiers and establish rules pertaining to the grant of licenses, thereby ensuring a systematic and controlled approach to dealing with potentially harmful substances.

The Poison Act of 1919 revolves around the restriction and regulation of the importation of specified poisons, aiming to safeguard of public health and safety by imposing necessary controls on the handling and transportation of such substances. The Act provides a legal framework to manage and monitor the importance of poisons, emphasizing the importance of obtaining licenses and adhering to prescribed conditions to prevent misuse or mishandling.

Objectives

- To ensure public safety by preventing the misuse and abuse of poisons, which can cause harm to human health and the environment
- To avoid the malpractice of poison in case of using it to kill a person or animal
- To avoid any sort of mischief
- To avoid self-medication by people, if the poison at certain dose is used in treatment
- To provide controlled medication by Registered Medical Practitioner.
- To prevent illegal sale of poisons in the country or from one country to another.
- To regulate import, possession & sale of poison in a specified country or whole area.
- To tighten the control over traffic in poison.

Possession and Sale of Poisons

Power of the State Government

The State Government is able to enact laws governing the sale and possession of any designated poison inside its borders. With the use of this authority, the

State Government can keep a close eye on and regulate the flow of potentially dangerous materials, protecting the health and welfare of its citizens. Furthermore, by using this power, the State Government can put policies in place to stop the improper use or abuse of these poisons, improving public health and lowering any possible dangers related to their sale.

Regulation of Possession for Sale

Any vendor or facility that has poisons for sale may be required by state government regulations to keep them in a safe custody, labelled containers, packages, or coverings, and inspect and examine the poisons. The legislation may also include procedures for licensing vendors or establishments engaged in the sale of specific poisons, as well as consequences for noncompliance. These steps are intended to protect the general public and stop the improper use or handling of potentially dangerous drugs.

Prohibition of Importation without a License

Unless and until a license is granted by the relevant authorities, the Central Government can prohibit the import of any poison into India. By ensuring that the import of poisons is strictly regulated and monitored, this precaution helps to prevent any potential misuse or harm to the general public. To further protect public safety, this licensing requirement enables the Central Government to keep control over the kinds and quantities of poisons introduced into the nation.

Presumption Regarding Designated Poisons

For the purposes of the Act, any substance that is listed as a poison in a rule established or notification issued under the Act is presumed to be a poison and is subject to the limitations and requirements set forth in the Act. In order to maintain public safety and avoid any potential injury or misuse, this includes the appropriate handling, storage, and transportation of such chemicals. This act gives the authority to the State Government to enforce the adherence to these rules and hold suppliers responsible for any violations.

Relation to Other Regulations

The Government of India has authority over the Poisons Act, 1919, and it has the authority to change or repeal it. The Act further states that the State of Jammu and Kashmir shall not be subject to its provisions, with the exception of those that deal with the import of any designated poison into India or the exportation of any specified poison from India. The Act also gives authority to the Central Government to establish regulations for enforcing its goals, such as those pertaining to the distribution, sale, importation, manufacturing, and possession of particular poisons.

Guidelines and Advisories

To guarantee adherence to the legal framework governing the retail sale of acids and chemicals, the Ministry of Home Affairs has sent advisories to administrators of industries covered by the MSIHC Rules from the Poisons Act, 1919. These recommendations cover precautions against misuse or unauthorized access to acids and chemicals, as well as safe handling, storage, and transportation practices. In order to safeguard public safety and avoid acid attacks and other dangerous situations using chemical substances, the Ministry of Home Affairs stresses how crucial it is to strictly follow these recommendations.

The State Government may rule or regulate within the whole or any part of the territories under its administration the possession and the sale, whether wholesale or retail of any poision.

In particular, and without prejudice to the generality of the foregoing power, such rules may provide for

(a) the grant of licenses to possess any specified poison for sale, wholesale or retail, and fixing of the fee (if any) to be charged for such license's;

(b) the classes of persons to whom alone such licenses may be granted;

(c) the classes of persons to whom alone any such poison may be sold;

(d) the maximum quantity of any such poison which may be sold to any one person;

(e) the maintenance of register of sale of any poison by the vendor,

(f) the safe custody of such poisons and the labelling of the vessels, packages or coverings in which any such poison is sold or possessed for sale; and

(g) the inspection and examination of any such poison when possessed for sale by any such vendor.

Import of Poisons

The Poisons Act of 1919 governs the import of poisons into India. The act grants the government to prohibit the entry of any poison into India unless a license or other specific authorization is obtained. This rule makes sure that the import of poisons is strictly regulated and monitored in order to stop abuse or illicit activity. To further protect the public's health and safety, the Poisons Act also requires stringent labelling and packaging regulations for imported poisons in order to ensure correct handling and storage. To safeguard animals and the agriculture sector, the Act also establishes restrictions on the possession of specific poison in areas where cow poisoning is a common occurrence. This clause permits local governments to closely monitor and control the possession of specified poison, ensuring that they are only used for legitimate purposes and not for malicious intent. By implementing these regulations, the government aims to maintain a safe and secure environment for both humans and animals in India.

- Central government gives license for import of poisons.
- Without license import of poisons is prohibited.
- Persons licensed to import poisons should follow all the conditions specified under the act.
- Poison must be imported across one of the defined customs frontiers.

Power to Prohibit Importation into India of any Poison Expect under License

- The Central Government has the authority, through an official notification in the Official Gazette, to restrict the importation of any designated poison across customs frontiers as defined by the Central Government.
- Such importation is permissible only under and in adherence to the conditions specified in a license. Additionally, the Central Government is empowered to establish rules governing the issuance of licenses for this purpose.

CHAPTER 8

Food Safety and Standards Authority of India (FSSAI)

Introduction

The Ministry of Health & Family Welfare, Government of India, established the Food Safety and Standards Authority of India (FSSAI), an independent authority. Under the Food Safety and Standards Act of 2006, which went into effect in 2006, it was established on August 5, 2011.

The FSSAI is in charge of overseeing and monitoring the processes used by food industry owners in the production, processing, storage, and packaging of food. To guarantee the safety and quality of food, it establishes standards for food items and grants permits and registrations.

The FSSAI is based in New Delhi and comprises 22 members, including a chairperson. It is the highest authority on food regulation in India and works to protect the general public's health by ensuring the availability of healthy, safe food.

The FSSAI also oversees the enforcement of various regulations related to food safety and standards in the country. These regulations include labelling requirements, hygiene practices, and permissible additives in food products.

The FSSAI regularly conducts inspections and audits of food establishments to ensure compliance with these regulations and takes necessary actions against non-compliant businesses. Additionally, the FSSAI also collaborates with other government agencies and stakeholders to promote awareness about food safety and encourage the adoption of best practices in the food industry.

The FSSAI has its headquarters at New Delhi. The authority also has 6 regional offices located in Delhi, Guwahati, Mumbai, Kolkata, Cochin, and Chennai.

FSSAI is headed by a non-executive chairperson appointed by the central government, who is either holding or has held the position of not below the rank of Secretary to the Government of India. The current chairperson of FSSAI is Sudhansh Pant and the current chief executive officer is Ganji Kamala V. Rao.

The organization has been set up as per the FSS Act 2006, until which different acts and laws were being administered under the various ministries of Government.

The Food Safety and Standards Act 2006

"An Act to consolidate the laws relating to food and to establish the Food Safety and Standards Authority of India for laying down science-based standards for articles of food and to regulate their manufacture, storage, distribution, sale and import, to ensure availability of safe and wholesome food for human consumption and for matters connected therewith or incidental thereto."

Functions of FSSAI

Following functions are performed by the Food Safety and Standards Authority of India-

***Framing Regulations*:** FSSAI formulates regulations to define standards and guidelines for food articles. These regulations cover safety, quality, and other relevant aspects.

***Accreditation of Certification Bodies*:** FSSAI establishes mechanisms and guidelines for accrediting certification bodies engaged in certifying food safety management systems for businesses.

***Laboratory Accreditation*:** FSSAI sets procedures and guidelines for accrediting laboratories. Accredited labs play a crucial role in ensuring food safety.

***Scientific Advice and Support*:** FSSAI provides scientific advice and technical support to the Central and State Governments. This support informs policy-making and rule-framing related to food safety and nutrition.

***Data Collection and Monitoring*:** FSSAI collects and collates data on food consumption, biological risks, contaminants, and emerging issues. It also facilitates a rapid alert system.

***Information Network*:** FSSAI creates an information network across the country, ensuring that the public, consumers, and local bodies receive reliable information about food safety.

The Main Aim of FSSAI

1. **Science-Based Standards:** FSSAI lays down science-based standards for articles of food. These standards cover aspects such as composition, quality, safety, and labelling.

2. **Regulation and Enforcement:** FSSAI regulates the manufacture, storage, distribution, sale, and import of food products. It ensures that food businesses adhere to the prescribed standards.
3. **Single Reference Point:** The Act aims to establish a single reference point for all matters related to food safety and standards. This shift streamlines control from multi-level, multi-departmental structures to a single line of command.
4. **Independent Authority:** FSSAI operates as an independent statutory authority with its head office in Delhi. It collaborates with State Food Safety Authorities to enforce provisions of the Act.

The FSSAI has established regulations for the manufacture, storage, sale, and labelling of food supplements. Here are some aspects related to these regulations:

Manufacture

The Food Safety and Standards (Health Supplements, Nutraceuticals, Food for Special Dietary Use, Food for Special Medical Purpose, Functional Food and Novel Food) Regulations, 2016 provide for the general conditions for manufacture of these foods.

The regulations specify that no person shall manufacture, pack, sell, offer for sale, market or otherwise distribute or import any food products referred to in these regulations without complying with all the provisions of these regulations.

The regulations also specify that the tablets, capsules, and syrups shall fulfill the general quality requirements and standards as specified in Indian Pharmacopoeia, British Pharmacopoeia, or United States Pharmacopoeia.

The FSSAI has also prepared a guidance document on Food Safety Management System (FSMS) to provide implementation guidance to food handlers involved in the food supplement supply chain.

Storage

The Food Safety and Standards (Health Supplements, Nutraceuticals, Food for Special Dietary Use, Food for Special Medical Purpose, Functional Food and Novel Food) Regulations, 2016 do not provide specific requirements related to the storage of food supplements.

However, the food business operators are required to comply with the general requirements for storage of food products as specified in the Food Safety and Standards (Licensing and Registration of Food Businesses) Regulations, 2011.

Sale

The Food Safety and Standards (Health Supplements, Nutraceuticals, Food for Special Dietary Use, Food for Special Medical Purpose, Functional Food and Novel Food) Regulations, 2016 provide requirements related to claims and labeling of food supplements.

The regulations specify that every package of food shall carry the name of the food, list of ingredients, and other information on the label as required under the Food Safety and Standards (Labelling and Display) Regulations, 2020.

The regulations also specify that the compliance to quantity of declared nutrients on the label shall be according to the established practices.

The food business operators are required to comply with the provisions of these regulations by 1st January 2018.

Labelling

The Food Safety and Standards (Health Supplements, Nutraceuticals, Food for Special Dietary Use, Food for Special Medical Purpose, Functional Food and Novel Food) Regulations, 2016 provide requirements related to labelling of food supplements.

The Food Safety and Standards (Labelling and Display) Regulations, 2020 prescribe the labelling requirements of pre-packaged foods and display of essential information on premises where food is sold.

The regulations specify that every pre-packaged food shall be labelled with information as required under these regulations unless otherwise provided.

The list of ingredients shall contain an appropriate title, such as the term "Ingredients/List of Ingredients".

The name of ingredients used in the product shall be listed in descending order of their composition by weight or volume, as the case may be at the time of its manufacture.

The regulations also specify that every package of food sold as a mixture or combination shall disclose the percentage of the ingredient used at the time of the manufacture of the food.

FSSAI has established comprehensive guidelines on the labelling of food products. According to these guidelines, the label of a food product should include the following information:

1. **Name of the food:** The name of the food product should be clearly displayed on the packaged product in a clear font.
2. **List of Ingredients:** The label must mention the elements used in making the final food product.

3. **Nutritional Information:** This should include details related to the calories, as well as other nutritional components of the food product.
4. **Declaration regarding Vegetarian or Non-Vegetarian:** The label should declare whether the product is vegetarian or non-vegetarian.
5. **Declaration regarding Food Additives:** Any food additives used in the product should be declared on the label.
6. **Net Quantity:** This refers to the weight of the product, including the weight of the product and the packaging weight combined.

These guidelines are mandatory for every packaged food item and are aimed at ensuring that consumers, traders, manufacturers, and investors are well-informed about the food products being sold. Adhering to these guidelines is essential to avoid fines, penalties, product recalls, or delays in product launches. The regulations also specify requirements for the labelling of pre-packaged foods and the display of processed, served, and stored foods. It is important to note that any information or pictorial device written, printed, or graphic matter on the label should be indelible and readily legible by the consumer under normal conditions of purchase and use.

CHAPTER 9

DPCO

Introduction

The Drug Price Control Order (DPCO) is a governmental directive issued under the Essential Commodities Act, empowering the government to set the prices for certain essential bulk drugs and their formulations. The roots of this control can be traced back to 1970, marking the initial instance when the government imposed restrictions on the profitability of pharmaceutical companies.

Objectives

- Ensuring the accessibility of essential, life-saving, and prophylactic medicines at affordable prices and of high quality.
- Promoting the rational utilization of drugs within the country and encouraging the cost-effective production of medicines with economically viable scales.

DPCO 2013

The government has implemented the Drug Price Control Order (DPCO) 2013 under the Essential Commodities Act, 1955, granting authority to the National Pharmaceutical Pricing Authority (NPPA) to regulate the prices of 348 essential drugs, including their specified strengths and dosages as per the National List of Essential Medicines (NLEM) 2011.

Main Features of the DPCO 2013

- ➢ The new order brings 348 drugs and their 652 formulations under price control.
- ➢ The pricing mechanism adopts a market-based approach, replacing the earlier proposed cost-plus method. The ceiling price is determined by calculating the simple average of prices for all brands of a drug with a market share of 1% or more.
- ➢ Wholesaler and retailer margins are reduced to 8% and 16%, respectively.

- Monitoring of the Maximum Retail Price (M.R.P) of Non-Scheduled formulations is emphasized.
- Control is exerted over Bulk Drug manufacturers.
- Oversight is extended to Formulation manufacturers.
- Drug producers are allowed an annual increase in the retail price in alignment with the Wholesale Price Index.

Scheduled Formulation

A scheduled formulation is defined as a formulation with the same strength and dosage form as specified in the schedule. If there is a change in the dosage form and strength of a scheduled formulation, it no longer qualifies as a scheduled drug.

Example:

- Amoxicillin Capsules 250mg is categorized under the schedule.
- However, Amoxicillin Tablet 125mg would not be classified as a scheduled drug if the dosage form and strength differ from the specified schedule.

Non - Scheduled Formulation

A "Non-Scheduled Formulation" refers to a formulation that includes a molecule whose dosage and strengths are not specified in the First Schedule. These formulations are not covered under the National List of Essential Medicines (Non-NLEM Drug/Formulation).

Examples include Aceclofenac, Norfloxacin, and Rabeprazole.

New Drug / New Formulation

A. Formulations listed in the National List of Essential Medicines (NLEM) that share the same specified dosage and strength, combined with other NLEM formulations having identical specified dosage and strength.

   Example:

   - A Paracetamol 500mg Tablet is categorized as a Scheduled Formulation.
   - A Diclofenac 50mg Tablet is also classified as a Scheduled Formulation.
   - The combination of Paracetamol 500mg and Diclofenac 50mg in a single tablet constitutes a New Drug/Formulation.

B. Formulations listed in the National List of Essential Medicines (NLEM) with the same specified dosage and strength, combined with other formulations not covered under NLEM.

Example:

- Paracetamol 500mg Tablet is a Scheduled Formulation.
- Aceclofenac 100mg Tablet is a Non-Scheduled Formulation.
- The combination of Paracetamol 500mg and Aceclofenac 100mg Tablet is considered a New Drug.

C. Formulations listed in the National List of Essential Medicines (NLEM) undergoing a change in strength.

Example:

- Paracetamol 500mg Tablet is a Scheduled Drug.
- Paracetamol 325mg Tablet is considered a New Drug.

D. Formulations listed in the National List of Essential Medicines (NLEM) undergoing a change in dosage.

Example:

- Diclofenac 50mg Tablet is a Scheduled Drug.
- Diclofenac 50mg Ointment is considered a New Drug.

Not considered a New Drug:

Example:

- Paracetamol 500mg is a Scheduled Drug.
- Aceclofenac 100mg is not a Scheduled Drug.
- The combination of Paracetamol 325mg and Aceclofenac 100mg is not a Scheduled Drug and does not require approval under DPCO for pricing.

Pricing of Scheduled Formulation

The determination of the ceiling price for a scheduled formulation with specified strengths and dosages, as outlined in the first schedule, involves the following steps:

Step 1: Calculation of Average Price to Retailer (P(s))

P(s) is the Average Price to Retailer for the scheduled formulation and is computed by dividing the sum of prices to the retailer for all brands and generic versions with a market share of one percent or more by the total number of such brands and generic versions based on their market turnover.

Step 2: Calculation of Ceiling Price (P(c))

P(c) is the Ceiling Price of the scheduled formulation and is determined by multiplying P(s) by (1+M/100), where M represents the margin to the retailer (16%).

Maximum Retail Price Calculation for Scheduled Formulations:

The Maximum Retail Price for scheduled formulations is set by manufacturers based on the government-notified Ceiling Price, plus applicable local taxes.

Maximum Retail Price = Ceiling Price + Local Taxes (if applicable)

Maximum Retail Price Calculation for New Drugs:

For new drugs, the Maximum Retail Price is established by manufacturers based on the government-determined Retail Price, plus applicable local taxes.

Maximum Retail Price = Retail Price + Local Taxes (if applicable)

Calculation of Retail Price for a Formulation:

Retail Price (R.P.) is determined by the government using the formula:

$$R.P. = (M.C. + C.C. + P.M. + P.C.) \times (1 + MAPE/100) + E.D.$$

Where:

- M.C. is the material cost, including the cost of drugs and other pharmaceutical aids.
- C.C. is the conversion cost calculated through established procedures.
- P.M. is the cost of packing material used in the formulation, including process loss.
- P.C. is the packing charges calculated using established costing procedures.
- MAPE (Maximum Allowable Post-manufacturing Expenses) represents all costs from ex-factory to retailing, including trade margin and manufacturer's margin, not exceeding one hundred percent for indigenously manufactured scheduled formulations.
- E.D. stands for excise duty, with special considerations for imported formulations.

Conclusion

- The cost of a 200 mg cefixime tablet is Rs. 23.84. Considering a Maximum Allowable Post-manufacturing Expenses (MAPE) of 100%, the basic price is calculated as Rs. 47.56 + 47.56 X 6.18% (Excise Duty, E.D.) = Rs. 50.49. However, as per the NPPA notification, the price for cefixime 200 mg is set at Rs. 112.50.
- For Ondansetron HCL injection with a cost of Rs. 2.13, applying a MAPE of 100%, the price becomes Rs. 4.26 + 4.26 X 6.18% (E.D.) = Rs. 4.52. In contrast, the NPPA notification establishes the price for ondansetron (2mg/ml) 1 ml at Rs. 7.37.

CHAPTER 10

Code of Ethics

Law

Law is defined as 'Rules of human conduct binding all persons in a state or nation'.

Ethics

Ethics is defined as Rules by which a profession regulates actions and sets standards for all its members.

LAW	ETHICS
Definition- Rules of human conduct binding on all persons in a state.	Definition- Rules by which a profession regulates action & sets standards for all its members.
Law may prevent one from causing injury to another, but it cannot force him to help his neighbour in hours of need.	Helping the neighbour is the function of ethics.
A law is something you must obey.	Ethics is how society expects you to behave.
Law deals with actions that are punishable.	Ethics deals with right & wrong.
Laws are written & approved documents.	Ethics are also written words, but they are not carrying legal status.
If law is broken, a violator may be subjected to punishment, a fine or imprisonment.	If rules of ethics are broken, the professional body may subject the violator to loss of professional privileges.

Pharmaceutical Code of Ethics

- Students in professional education must become competent in their profession. so, he must be able to place his skills within the context of society.
- Every professional practitioner needs social understanding to do his work well.
- Therefore, it is the duty of all those involved in pharmacy field to be sure that the pharmacist in training knows the standards of professional

conduct (code of ethics) and understands that deviation from those standards cannot maintain the status of pharmacy profession.

- Pharmacy being a profession requires knowledge skill and integrity on the part of those engaged in it.
- This profession is associated with medical profession in the responsible duties of preserving the public health.
- Also, it deals with dispensing the useful and sometimes useful and dangerous agent to cure the diseases.
- Pharmacy council of India has formulated the code of ethics for the guidance of pharmacist.
- Such code of ethics covers the rules or the principles to be observed by the pharmacist while dealing himself with his job.

Pharmacist in Relation to His Job

Pharmaceutical Services

- A pharmacist should provide efficient and reasonably comprehensive pharmaceutical services through the medical store or pharmacy.
- Such services should include supply of commonly required medicines without undue delay and always furnishing the emergency supply.

Pharmacy/Drug Store

- In every pharmacy/ drug store, there should be qualified pharmacist to have personal control over the pharmacy.
- A pharmacy should be planned in such a way that there is no accidental contamination in the preparation, dispensing and supply of medicines.
- The appearance of the premises should reflect the professional character of pharmacy.

Prescriptions

- Prescriptions presented for dispensing should not be discussed with patients or others regarding the merits and demerits of their therapeutic efficiency.
- A pharmacist should not show any expression on his face so that the patients will lose their faith in the physicians or prescribers after receiving the prescriptions.
- No addition, omission or substitution of ingredients in a Rx should be made without the consent of prescriber whenever possible except in an emergency.

- In case of any error in the prescription, it should be referred to the prescriber for necessary correction or approval of the change suggested.
- If at all change in the prescription is necessary, it should not affect the reputation of physician.
- A pharmacist should not recommend any particular prescriber unless he is specially asked to do so.

Drugs/Ingredients

- While dispensing, the drugs or ingredients should be weighed or measured correctly.
- Pharmacist should always use drugs and medicinal preparations of standard quality.
- Drugs likely to cause addiction or abuse should not be supplied when there is reason to suppose that it is required for such purpose.

Practical Training

- While imparting practical training, the in-charge pharmacist should see that the trainees acquire sufficient technique and skill.
- No certificate should be granted to the trainee pharmacist before completion of prescribed period of training or without undergoing practical training or unless the trainee acquires sufficient knowledge.

Pharmacist in Relation to His Trade

Price Structure

- Prices charged from customers should be fair and in keeping with the quality of drugs & medical preparations supplied.
- The compounding & dispensing charges should be fair & without unduly taxing the purchaser.

Fair Trade Practices

- No attempt should be made to capture the business of a fellow pharmacist by cutthroat competition, i.e., by offering reduced price, prizes or gifts.
- Labels, trademarks, symbols and other signs of fellow pharmacist should not be copied.
- Drugs or other ingredients required should always be purchased from reputable source.

Hawking of Drugs

- Hawking of drugs and medicinal should not be allowed.
- Any attempt should not be made to collect the orders from door to door.

- Self-servicing method in pharmacy or drug - stores should not be allowed as it may encourage self-medication which is undesirable & dangerous.

Advertising and Displays

- No display or advertisement on the premises, in the newspaper or elsewhere regarding the abilities & services provided by the pharmacy.
- Pharmacist should not make such advertisement which contains:
  - Misleading, or exaggerated statements or claims.
  - The word "Cure" in reference to an ailment or symptoms of ill-health.
  - A guarantee of therapeutic efficacy.
  - An appeal to fear.
  - An offer to refund money paid.
  - A prize, competition or similar scheme.
  - A reference to sexual weakness, premature ageing.

Pharmacist in Relation to Medical Profession

- A pharmacist under no circumstances, should practice medicine, that is diagnosing diseases and prescribing medicines. However, in case of accidents or emergencies, he may render first aid services.
- A pharmacist should not recommend any medical practitioner, unless specially asked for.
- Pharmacist should never enter into secret agreements with the medical profession, physicians, dentist, and veterinary surgeons to offer them commission or gifts by recommending his dispensary or drug store.
- Pharmacist should not have any clandestine or underhand arrangement with any physician.
- Pharmacist is a link between medical profession and public. He should be constantly in touch with the modern developments in pharmacy and allied fields. He should be expert in the field of pharmacy so that he may advice the physician on pharmaceutical matters. By enlarging his store of knowledge, he may be able to educate the public to maintain their health.
- Pharmacists should neither discuss physician's prescription with customers nor disclose to them the composition of the prescriptions.

Pharmacist in Relation to His Profession

- A pharmacist should observe the law and ethical principles to maintain the standard of the profession.

- A pharmacist should extend the help and co-operation to his fellow pharmacist in an emergency and legitimate needs.
- A pharmacist should try to weed out the undesirable corrupt or dishonest conduct of the member of his profession maintaining its status in society.
- A pharmacist should have a fair knowledge of laws of the state and nation pertaining to food, drug, pharmacy education, health etc.
- A pharmacist should have an upto date knowledge of professional matters. It should associate himself with various pharmaceutical organizations, the aims and objects of which are compatible with this code of ethics.
- A pharmacist should not perform such acts which will bring discredit to his profession or to himself.

Pharmacist's OATH

- I swear by the code of ethics of Pharmacy Council of India, in relation to the community and shall act as an integral part of health care team.
- I shall uphold the laws and standards governing my profession.
- I shall strive to perfect and enlarge my knowledge to contribute to the advancement of pharmacy and public health.
- I shall follow the system which I consider best for Pharmaceutical care and counseling of patients.
- I shall endeavor to discover and manufacture drugs of quality to alleviate sufferings of humanity.
- I shall hold in confidence the knowledge gained about the patients in connection with my professional practice and never divulge unless compelled to do so by the law.
- I shall associate with organizations having their objectives for betterment of the profession of Pharmacy and make contribution to carry out the work of those organizations.
- While I continue to keep this oath unviolated, may it be granted to me to enjoy life and the practice of pharmacy respected by all, at all times !
- Should I trespass and violate this oath, may the reverse be my lot!

CHAPTER 11

Medical Termination of Pregnancy Act and Rules

Induction of Abortion

- Deliberate termination of pregnancy before the viability of fetus is called induction of abortion.
- Induced abortion can be legal or illegal (criminal).
- Until the MTP act was passed, proving abortion remained punishable under Indian law.
- In case of death due to abortion procedure there was punishment of upto 10 years imprisonment and fine.
- In India, abortion was legalized by medical termination of pregnancy MTP act 1971 and enforced in 1972 and provisions were revised in 1975.

MTP Act: Addressing a Public Health Priority

Since legalization of abortion in India, deliberate induction of abortion by RMP(Registered Medical Practitioner) in interest of mothers health and life is protected under the MTP act.

MTP Act and Aims

- Aims to improve the maternal health scenario by preventing large number of unsafe abortions and consequent high incidence of maternal mortality & morbidity.
- Legalizes abortion services.
- Promotes access to safe abortion services to women.
- De-criminalizes the abortion seeker.
- Offers protection to medical practitioners who otherwise would be penalized under the Indian Penal Code (sections 315-316).

Legal Framework

MTP Act

- Lays down when & where pregnancies can be terminated.

- Grants the central government power to make rules and the state government power to frame regulations.

MTP Rules

- Lays down who can terminate the pregnancy, training requirements, approval process for place, etc.

MTP Regulations

- Lays down forms for opinion, maintenance of records.
- Custody of forms and reporting of cases.

MTP Act: Place for Conducting MTP

- A hospital established or maintained by Government.
- A place approved for the purpose of this Act by a District-level Committee constituted by the government with the CMHO as Chairperson.

MTP Act Amendment 2002

- MTP amendment act was passed in 2002.
- Term Lunatic was replaced by – Mentally ill.
- MTP place to be approved by a district level committee chaired by CMO / DHO.
- Defaulters- rigorous punishment for 2-7 year.
- Owner of the place also responsible if defaulter.

Implications of Amendments

- Simplifies registration of sites which can be done at district level now.
- Providers can get their sites approved for providing abortions under the MTP Act for 1st trimester only or up to 20 weeks and thereby come under the protective cover of the MTP Act.
- Approved providers can provide medical abortions from their clinic, as long as they have access to an approved site.
- Offers potential to increase number of approved sites, which would enable women to access safe abortion services.
- Effective implementation will help to bring all abortions within legal frame work.

MTP Rules: What do they Cover?

- Experience & training required for providers.
- Approval of a place for terminating pregnancy under the Act.

- ➢ Composition & tenure of District Level Committee.
- ➢ Inspection, cancellation or suspension of approval; review.
- ➢ Consent form.

MTP Rules: Who Can Perform?

A medical practitioner (RMP) .

- Who has a recognized medical qualification
- Whose name has been entered in a State Medical Register and
- Who has such experience or training in Gynecology and Obstetrics as prescribed by Rules made under the Act

CHAPTER 12

Government Pharma Regulatory Bodies

Role of Regulatory Bodies

1. To ensure safety, efficacy & quality of drugs available to the public.
2. To identify strengths & weakness of drug regulation & to propose strategies to improve drug regulation.
3. To ensure & increase regulatory implementation in non-regulated parts of the world for safety of people.

Regulatory Bodies of Some Country

Sr. no	Country	Regulatory body
1	India	Central Drug Standard Control Organization. (CDSCO)
2	USA	Food and Drug Administration (FDA)
3	Japan	Ministry of Health, Labour and Welfare. (MHLW)

Central Drug Standard Control Organization (CDSCO)

The CDSCO is a national regulatory authority of India has 379 staff members & they works under Directorate General of Health Service of Ministry of Health & Family Welfare.

The heads of CDSCO is Drug controller General of India (DCGI).

There are 6 zonal offices, 4 sub-zonal offices, 13 port offices, 7 laboratories under the control of CDSCO.

CDSCO approves drugs & conduct of clinical trials, set standard for drugs , control quality of imported drugs in India & coordinates the activities of State Drug Control Organizations.

CDSCO & State regulators together grant licenses for some specialized class of critical drugs, such as blood, blood products, I.V fluids, Vaccines & sera.

They rise in recruitment & staffing of CDSCO has occurred from 111 positions in April 2008 to 474 positions at the current time.

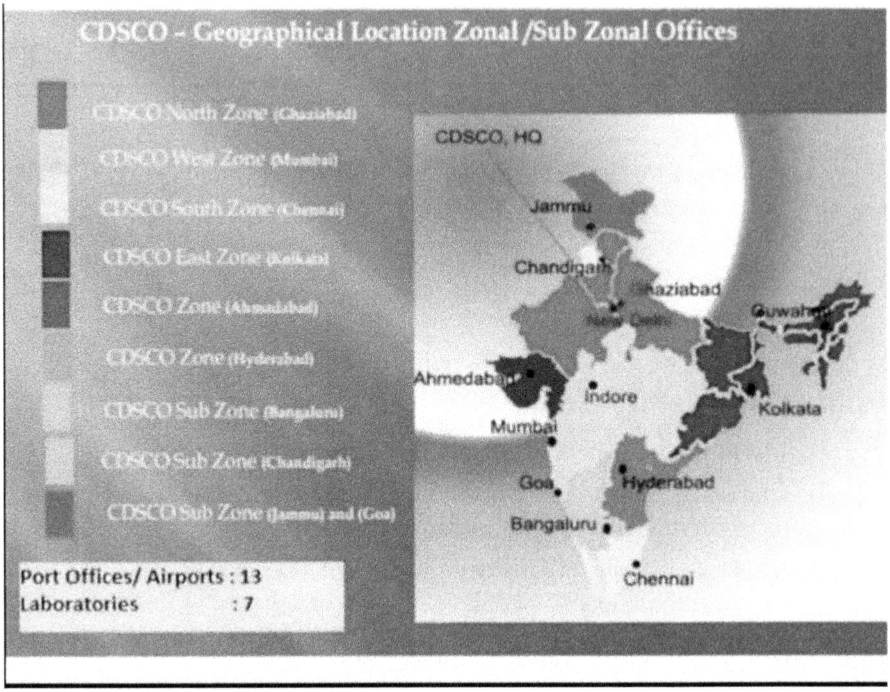
CDSCO - Geographical Location Zonal /Sub Zonal Offices
CDSCO North Zone (Ghaziabad)
CDSCO West Zone (Mumbai)
CDSCO South Zone (Chennai)
CDSCO East Zone (Kolkata)
CDSCO Zone (Ahmadabad)
CDSCO Zone (Hyderabad)
CDSCO Sub Zone (Bangaluru)
CDSCO Sub Zone (Chandigarh)
CDSCO Sub Zone (Jammu) and (Goa)
Port Offices/ Airports : 13
Laboratories : 7
CDSCO, HQ
Jammu
Chandigarh
Ghaziabad
Ahmedabad
Indore
Mumbai
Kolkata
Goa
Hyderabad
Bangaluru
Chennai

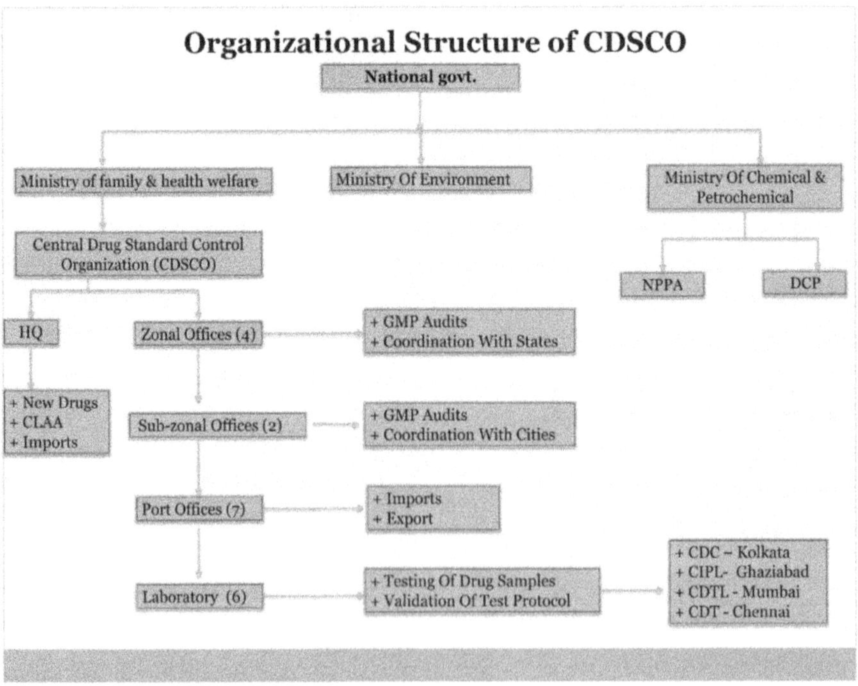
Organizational Structure of CDSCO
National govt.
Ministry of family & health welfare
Ministry Of Environment
Ministry Of Chemical & Petrochemical
Central Drug Standard Control Organization (CDSCO)
NPPA
DCP
HQ
Zonal Offices (4)
+ GMP Audits
+ Coordination With States
+ New Drugs
+ CLAA
+ Imports
Sub-zonal Offices (2)
+ GMP Audits
+ Coordination With Cities
Port Offices (7)
+ Imports
+ Export
Laboratory (6)
+ Testing Of Drug Samples
+ Validation Of Test Protocol
+ CDC - Kolkata
+ CIPL- Ghaziabad
+ CDTL - Mumbai
+ CDT - Chennai

Functions of CDSCO

- Testing of New Drugs, Oversight & Market Surveillance through Inspectorate of Centre over and above the State Authority
- Approving Of Blood Banks, Vaccines, r- DNA Products & Some Medical Devices (CLAA Scheme)
- Amendment to D & C Act & Rules Banning of Drugs & Cosmetics Grant of Test License, Personal License, NOCs, for Export Testing of New Drugs Oversight & Market Surveillance through Inspectorate of Centre Over and above the State Authority
- It makes policies & procedure for uniform implementation of the provisions of Drugs & Cosmetics Act, 1940 & Rules, 1945.
- It assists in setting & implementation of standard for drugs, cosmetics & medical devices.
- It coordinated & interacts with international organizations like WHO, U.S., FDA, European Medicines Agency (EMA), Pharmaceuticals & Medical Devices Agency (PMDA) of Japan, European Directorate for Quality of Medicines & HealthCare (EDQM), South Asian Association for Regional Cooperation (SAARC), WHO Regional Office for South East Asia (SEARO) BRICS nations (Brazil, Russia, India, China & South Africa), etc.
- It controls import of medicines, approval of new medicines & clinical trials, conduct of meetings with Drugs Consultative Committee (DCC) & Drugs Technical Advisory Board (DTAB), & Function As Central License Approving Authority (CLAA) for approval of certain licenses.
- It maintains drugs testing laboratories for sample testing.
- It performs inspections along with Zonal Offices & coordinate actions with state Drugs Controllers under their authority.

Indian Pharmacopoeia Commission (IPC)

1. The Indian Pharmacopoeia (IPC) is an autonomous institution under the Ministry of Health & Family Welfare of Indian government.
2. IPC was established to create drugs standards in the country.
3. IPC issue official documentation in the form of Indian Pharmacopoeia (IP) to improve the quality of medicines by adding new & updating old monographs.
4. It also publishes the National Formulary of India, which encourage the rational use of generic pharmaceuticals.
5. IP Reference Substances (IPRS) are provided by IPC & operate as a fingerprint for identifying a product under test & its purity as specified in IP.

6. IP establishes standards for identity, purity & strength of medications that are crucial for human & animal health care.

Structure of IPC Indian

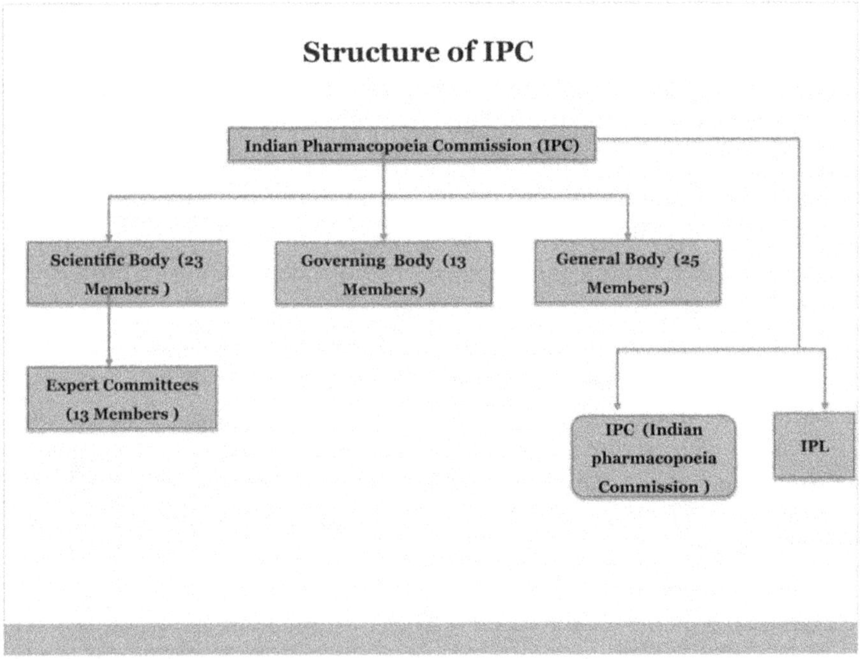

Pharmacopoeia Commission (IPC), Scientific Body (23 Members), Governing Body (13 Members), General Body (25 Members), Expert Committees (13 Members), IPC (Indian pharmacopoeia Commission) IPL.

1. The IPC began operations as an autonomous institution on 1st January 2009, under administrative control of Ministry of Health & Family Welfare, India.
2. The chief Scientific & Executive Officer is the Secretary cum Scientific Director.
3. The IPC is organized into three levels, i.e., the General body, the governing body, & the Scientific body, having professionals from diverse fields of science & technology.

Objectives

1. To improve public & animal health in India by establishing authoritative & officially recognized quality standard for drugs, including Active Pharmaceutical Ingredients (APIs), excipients and dosage forms used by health professionals, patients & consumers.

2. To promote highest standards of drugs for human & animal consumption, within the practical limits of manufacturing & analysing technologies.

Functions of IPC

1. Publishing a new edition & addendums of the Indian Pharmacopoeia.
2. Publishing the National Formulary of India.
3. Functioning as National Coordination Centre (NCC) for operating Indian Pharmacovigilance Program (PvPI).
4. Forming working relationship with other national & international institutions having similar positions.
5. Providing certification & dissemination of IP Reference Substances.

CHAPTER 13

Good Regulatory Practices

Introduction

Good regulatory practices: it is the role of government to protect and promote public health and safety by delivering appropriate health care to its people. For this, the assurance of functioning health care requires safe, affordable, and effective medical products. The safety and efficacy of health products are assured by entrusted regulatory bodies like the USFDA in the USA and CDSCO in India. These regulatory authorities authorize the export, import, and marketing approval of assured quality medical products. Thus, safeguarding the public health. The constantly changing regulatory system can be recognized from the 67th World Health Assembly which under WHA 67.20 took the resolution of strengthening the regulatory system for medical products. Good Regulatory Practices are mandatory for the sound working of regulatory bodies. GRP is defined as processes and tools to improve the quality and effectiveness of regulations for sectors like medical products, health, and trade. GRP ensures that regulations are transparent, clear, consistent, proportionate, impartial, timely, and science-based. these also promote greater contribution and collaboration among regulatory authorities at national and international levels.

Some benefits of GRP are:

- To protect and promote the health and safety of the public and environment.
- Reduce unnecessary trade barriers to trade and innovation.
- Enhance trust of public and regulatory system confidence.
- Improve efficiency and performance of the regulatory system.

Principles of GRP

- ***Legality:*** Regulations passed based on clear legal mandate and should comply with the rules of law.
- ***Independence:*** The behavior of regulators should be impartial and integral and without any undue influence or interference.

- ***Consistency:*** Regulatory officers should be coherent and compatible with planned rules and regulations.
- ***Clarity:*** The regulations planned and implemented should be clear, simple, and easy to understand and comply. The scope of the subject which the regulation should be clear.
- ***Flexibility:*** The regulations should be adaptable and responsive to any change in circumstances and new evidence.
- ***Proportionality:*** Regulations should be adjusted to achieve policy objectives and prevent any excessive burdens and costs.
- ***Transparency:*** The development of regulation should be developed and implemented in a consultative and participatory manner giving access to relevant information and feedback opportunities.
- ***Efficiency:*** The development and implementation of regulation should be done in a timely and cost-effective manner to avoid duplication and overlapping.

Various Parts under Good Regulatory Practices (GRP)

Documentation

Documentation is a vital part of quality control which provides evidence of compliance of one process, product, and facility with GRP requirements. The documentation should follow the ALCOA and ALCOA-plus principles of attributable documentation (clear identification of data along with information on who and when the process was conducted), Legible documentation (Easy understandability and readability of data by reviewer), Original documenttation (Primary/original data record should be maintained), Contemporaneous document (data recorded while the activity is being performed), Accurate documentation (data recorded is error-free and reflects actual outcomes) and documentation (data compiled should be complete, enduring, consistent and available). Some types of documentation required under GRP are Procedures: written instructions on steps to perform various activities and processes Examples include Standard Operating Procedure (SOP), and protocol/guidelines. Reports: documents comprising summarisation/analysis of data from records like validation reports, risk assessment reports, and stability reports. Records: documents providing execution evidence of procedure/results like a batch record, certificate of analysis, and test report. All documents should be prepared, reviewed, approved, distributed, stored, and archived in a controlled manner as per SOP and requirements of regulatory authorities. All documents should be prepared, maintained, and archived as per good documentation practices.

Community Pharmacy

The Health Professions Act (HPA) Bylaws mandate that all prescriptions in community pharmacy, including both new and refill prescriptions, must include written confirmation of the registrant who verified the patient identification, verified the patient allergy information, and reviewed the personal health information on PharmaNet.

Hospital Pharmacy

The American Society of Health-System Pharmacy (ASHP) has published guidelines for minimum standards for pharmacies in hospitals. These guidelines outline a minimum level of services that most hospital pharmacy departments should consistently provide. The guidelines cover a range of topics, including management of practice, development of medication-use policy, medication therapy optimization, procurement of drug product and inventory management, preparing, packaging, and labelling medications, medication delivery, monitoring medication use, evaluating the effectiveness of the medication-use system, and research.

WHOLESALE: Selling items to customer without any retailer at reasonable price in large quantities.

Main documents required as per regulatory standards: FDA 21 CFR Part 11, FDA Guidance for Industry Data Integrity Compliance with Drug cGMP, EMA Good Manufacturing Practice (GMP) guidance to ensure Data Integrity, MHRA Data Integrity Guidance and Definitions, WHO Guideline on Data Integrity, Annex 4, PIC/S Good Practices for Data Management and Integrity in Regulated GMP/GDP Environments.

Licenses are permission/authorization obtained officially granted by competent regulatory authorities to conduct certain activities like development, distribution, manufacture, import, export, marketing, and use of regulated products like drugs, cosmetics, food, and medical devices. License is only issued after assessment of the applicant's compliance with legislation, standards, policies, scientific, administrative, and ethical requirements. the licenses need to be subjected to renewal, inspection, and monitoring to ensure constant compliance with regulatory standards and guidelines.

Licenses Required under GRP

- **Manufacturing license:** License authorized for regulated product production using good manufacturing practices (GMP) and other quality standards. This license also specifies scope, scale, and location of product activities along with responsibilities and manufacturer obligations.

- **Product license:** A license which authorises the applicant to manufacture and sale of regulated product in a specific area based on the quality, efficacy, and safety evaluation of the product. It also specifies use conditions, indications, contraindications, precautions, warnings, and adverse reactions of licensed products.
- **Import License:** License authorizing the entry of regulated products into a jurisdiction based on import regulations and procedures compliance. It also specifies the source, origin, and quality of the product to be imported and customer and clearance requirements that need to be fulfilled.
- **Distribution license:** license authorizing storage, transport, and delivery of regulated product from vendor/manufacturer to customer/end-user after compliance with GDP (Good Distribution Practices) and other supply standards. It also specifies types, quantities, and destinations to which product needs to be delivered along with maintenance of records and reports.
- **Export License:** license authorizing exit of regulated product from a jurisdiction only after complying with export regulations and procedures. It also specifies the location, purpose, and quantity of product to be exported and export documentation, and certification to be provided.

Renewals

Under GRP, renewals are defined as the process of reviewing and updating the validity and quality of regulations previously issued/adopted. It helps ensure that regulations remain effective, efficient, and relevant without imposing unnecessary burdens/costs on the public. these also facilitate international trade and cooperation by reducing regulatory divergences in different jurisdictions. some practices under GRP supporting renewals are the establishment of clear criteria and procedures for the identification and selection of regulations that need to be renewed based on impact, performance, relevance, and stakeholder feedback. Regular and systemic reviews of existing regulations using evidence-based methods like regulatory impact assessment, and reliance on global standards. This promotes coordination and cooperation with regulatory authorities at national and international levels avoiding duplication, and conflicts of regulations to promote harmonization and mutual recognition. Also provides the public and stakeholders with transparent and timely information on renewal processes, rationale and objectives of proposed changes, benefits expected, and costs as per renewed regulations. Under the process of renewals, the evaluation of outcomes and impacts of renewed regulations is also covered along with a collection of feedback for further improvement.

Applications forms using which grant and renewal of license can be done:

Application Type	Description
Form 14A	Application from a purchaser for test or analysis of a drug under Section 26 of the Drugs and Cosmetics Act, 1940
Form 19	Application for grant or renewal of a licence to sell, stock, exhibit or offer for sale, or distribute drugs other than those specified in Schedule X
Form 19A	Application for grant or renewal of a restricted licence to sell, stock or exhibit or offer for sale, or distribute drugs by retail by dealers who do not engage the service of a qualified person
Form 19B	Application for licence to sell, stock or exhibit or offer for sale, or distribute Homoeopathic Medicines.
Form 19C	Application for grant or renewal of a (licence to sell, stock, exhibit or offer for sale, or distribute) drugs specified in Schedule X
Form 24	Application for the grant of or renewal of a licence to manufacture for sale or for distribution of drugs other than those specified in (Schedule C, C (1) and X)
Form 24A	Application for grant or renewal of a loan licence to manufacture for sale or for distribution of drugs other than those specified in Schedule C, C (1) and X
Form 24B	Application for grant or renewal of a licence to repack for sale or distribution of drugs, being drugs other than those specified in Schedule C and C (1) excluding those specified in Schedule X
Form 24C	Application for the grant or renewal of a licence to manufacture for sale (or for distribution) of Homoeopathic medicines or a licence to manufacture potentised preparations from back potencies by licensees holding licence in Form 20-C
Form 24F	Application for grant or renewal of a licence to manufacture for sale or for distribution of drugs specified in Schedule X and not specified in Schedule C and C (1).
Form 27	Application for grant or renewal of a licence to manufacture for sale or for distribution of drugs specified in Schedule C and C (1) excluding those specified in part XB and Schedule X
Form 27A	Application for grant or renewal of a loan licence to manufacture for sale or for distribution of drugs specified in Schedule C and C (1) excluding those specified in part XB and Schedule X
Form 27B	Application for grant or renewal of a licence to manufacture for sale or for distribution of drugs specified in Schedules C, C (1) and X.
Form 27C	Application for grant/renewal of licence for the operation of a Blood Bank for processing of whole blood and / or preparation of blood components.
Form 27D	Application for grant or renewal of a licence to manufacture for sale or for distribution of Large Volume Parenterals/Sera and Vaccines excluding those specified in Schedule X
Form 27DA	Application for grant or renewal of a loan licence to manufacture for sale or for distribution of large volume parenterals/sera and vaccine/recombinant DNA (R-DNA) derived drugs excluding those specified under Schedule X

Table *Contd..*

Application Type	Description
Form 27E	Application for grant /renewal* of licence to manufacture Blood products for sale or distribution
Form 27F	Application for grant or renewal of licence.
Form 30	Application for licence to manufacture drugs for purpose of examination, test or analysis
Form 31	Application for grant or renewal of a licence to manufacture cosmetics for sale or for distribution
Form 31A	Application for grant or renewal of a loan licence to manufacture cosmetics for sale (or for distribution)
Form 36	Application for grant or renewal of approval for carrying out tests drugs/cosmetics or raw materials used in the manufacture thereof on behalf of licensees for manufacture for sale of drugs/ cosmetics.
Form 44	Application for grant of permission to import or manufacture a New Drug or to undertake clinical trial.

E-governance

E-governance is a system of governance that uses Information and Communications Technology (ICT) to carry out government functions and achieve results. The primary goal of e-governance is to ensure that all citizens have equal access to public services and the benefits of economic growth, while also ensuring transparency and accountability in government activities. India has made significant strides in e-governance, with initiatives such as the National e-Governance Plan (NeGP) and Digital India driving the country's digital transformation. The NeGP is a program designed to integrate and improve e-governance initiatives across the country, to make public services more accessible and citizen-centric. The program includes 31 Mission Mode Projects (MMPs) and 8 components and aims to increase the reach of government services both geographically and demographically. However, implementing e-governance poses several challenges, such as building capacity within the government, raising awareness about e-governance among citizens, and changing the government's processes, outlook, laws, rules, and regulations.

Inspections

These are defined as inspecting a premises for licensing by checking if the processes and premises meet the standards as per the GRP standards. Inspections are conducted only after application submission by the applicant. they are scheduled prior and can be surprise visits or known visits. during inspections, inspectors are empowered to take proofs, and samples and inspect any document, personnel, and part of the premises. After inspection, inspectors compile a report showing the status of the inspection. Based on these reports the regulatory authority authorizes the applicant.

Import and export of drugs and medical devices: Import is defined as ordering drugs or medical devices from other countries and export is defined as selling drugs and medical devices to some other country. The requirement of customer clearance and regulatory compliance is essential for import and export. For the export of medical devices, a No Objection Certificate (NOC) is required as per CDSCO regulations.

CHAPTER 14

Introduction to BCS System

Introduction

The Biopharmaceutical classification system was developed in 1995. It is the way to classify the drugs based on their solubility and permeability. According to BCS system the drugs are classified into four categories:

BCS Class I includes those drugs which have highly solubility and highly permeability. Hence these drugs get easily dissolved and absorbed by blood stream. Examples: Metoprolol, Propanolol, Diltiazem, Caffeine and Ibuprofen.

BCS Class II includes those drugs which have poor solubility and high permeability. These kinds of drugs absorb rapidly but dissolve slowly. Bioavailability can be controlled by controlling dosage form and rate of release of drug substance. Examples: Nifedipine, Naproxen, Ketoconazole and Danazol.

BCS Class III includes those drugs which have high solubility and poor permeability. These drugs are easily dissolved but their absorbance is hindered. Examples: Metformin, Insulin, Atenolol and Cimetidine.

BCS Class IV includes those drugs which have low solubility and low permeability. These drugs are neither dissolved nor absorbed so an alternative route other than oral route is needed. Examples: Taxol, Chlorthiazole, Cefixime, Griseofulvin and Diazepam.

Basic Concepts of Clinical Trials

Clinical trials are performed to check the efficacy and safety of drugs on humans after their efficacy and safety have been proved in pre-clinical studies. These are performed on human volunteers to find new treatments or to replace the existing treatments with some other effective systems. Based upon the aim of trials clinical trials can be classified as treatment trial which deals with testing of new combination of drugs, prevention trials where drug is tested to look for its ability to prevent disease and quality of life trial which is performed to find the ways to improve quality of life in chronic disease. These studies are part of research studies that aim to find how a drug or medical treatment shows action in humans. There are 4 phases of clinical trials:

Phase I trials include 20 to 100 volunteers with the aim to establish a maximum dose which is safe and tolerable. Before beginning with phase I trials a phase 0 called as micro dosing is also performed in which a drug is administered to a small group of patients and in a very low dose in order to ascertain the pharmacokinetic properties of drugs.

Phase II trials also termed as exploratory trials include 100 to 150 patients with the aim to establish a therapeutic efficiency and dose ranging.

Phase III trials also termed as confirmatory trials include a large number of patients from various centers to ensure the same therapeutic efficiency is observed in different population.

Phase IV trials also called post marketing surveillance where the drug is released in the market for consumption and is monitored for specific time to look for any kind of side effects. If side effects occur then the drug is withdrawn form market by initiating the drug recall mechanism.

Before performing a clinical trial an informed consent is to be filled by the participants that provide them the information about the kind of treatment they are undergoing and know all the possible side effects and risk associated with its exposure. Studies are usually performed in randomization, where participants in clinical trials are randomly assigned to treatment and control groups.

Abbreviated New Drug Application (ANDA)

- It is the type of the application to be sent to the U.S. Food and Drug Administration (FDA) for seeking approval for the marketing of generic drugs. It is only after the approval of application that an applicant can start manufacturing and marketing of generic drugs. Since these applications are required for the generic drugs which are alternative to branded drugs so they do not require any data of pre-clinical or clinical trials.
- The main goals of ANDA are to reduce the cost of drug by providing these generic drugs and to increase the bioavailability of drug in comparison to reference listed drugs. The ANDA was established in 1970 by FDA for review and approval of generic drugs. ANDA ensures that the product meets the identity, strength, quality and purity standards. Both efficacy and safety are equivalent to that of branded product. In order to fill ANDA certain information is required like information related to product, manufacturing procedure, testing facilities, dissolution profile, labeling and control procedures.

NDA (New Drug Application)

- New drug application is another type of application which is to be submitted to U.S FDA to seek permission for marketing of new drug. Unlike the ANDA, NDA requires the data of clinical and preclinical data for its approval. The data about procedure of clinical trial, results of pre-clinical studies, pharmacokinetics, manufacturing, processing and packaging of drug are required in NDA.
- The main goal of NDA is to provide sufficient information about the drug which will ensure its safety and efficacy and at the same time will permit FDA to review whether the drug is safe, whether labeling is appropriate and also the methods used in manufacturing of drug adhere to quality standards.

New Drug Development

- The process of development of drug is complicated and time consuming as a lot of research work is required beginning from the identification of drug targets to the steps to modify these targets to achieve desired action. It takes approximately 15 to 20 years for bringing a drug molecule into the market. The new drug development entails the process of research, pre-clinical, clinical trials, post marketing surveillance and regulatory approval.
- The process of drug development includes 3 main phases drug discovery, drug development and FDA review. The drug discovery phase includes discovering the drug which is effective and safe. The drug development includes synthesis of drug in such a form which is easily approved and acceptable for the marketing. The last phase is review by FDA; the FDA can approve the drug, reject the approval or can demand for certain additional information may be required for approving the drug.

New Drug and Clinical Trial Rules, (NDCT) 2019

- The new drug and clinical trials rules of 2019 provides faster accessibility of new drugs. These new rules promote the research throughout the country and supersede part XA and Schedule Y of the Drugs and Cosmetic Rules, 1945. There are 13 chapters listed in the new rules with total 107 rules and 8 schedules, each chapter deals with certain aspects.
- The certain changes are brought by new rules in comparison to previous NDCT rules like change in provision of compensation, change in responsibility of ethical committee and the time line for regulatory approval has been reduced.
- In case of serious adverse effects, investigator shall forward the report to sponsor and Ethical Committee. Ethical Committee within the period of

30 days shall decide the compensation and pass their orders to investigator.

- To manufacture a new drug permission is to be obtained from central licensing authority, thus if the permission is granted it is valid for tenure of 3 years.
- The Drug Controller is designated as Central Licensing Authority, to act as nodal entity for licensing and approval as per these rules.

Brand v/s Generic Drugs

Features	Generic Drugs	Brand Drugs
1. Definition	Generic drugs are manufactured only after the expiry of patent.	Brand drugs are marketed, manufactured and protected under the patent.
2. Price	Cheaper in comparison to brand drugs.	Have a higher cost.
3. Type of Application	It requires ANDA for its approval.	It requires NDA for approval.
4. Studies	No preclinical and clinical study required to establish safety and efficacy of drug.	Requires results of both preclinical and clinical data for its approval.
5. Excipients	Either the same or altered excipients are present.	Only acceptable excipients by the innovator company are used for their production.
6. Example	Paracetamol tablet	Tylenol, Para, NAPA, Mapap.

Trade Name Concept

Trade name is also called as "business name" or "doing business as" (DBA). Trade name is a company's name provided to distinguish its products from other business. To ensure the names are not copied or used by other individuals they are often registered with government. In simple words, trade name is the name used by company to conduct their business.

Introduction to Patent Law

- A patent is an exclusive right granted for an invention, whether it's a product or a process, which presents an innovative approach to achieve a goal or offers a new technical solution to a problem. To secure a patent, comprehensive technical details about the invention must be disclosed to the public through a patent application.
- The history of patent law in India dates back to 1911 with the enactment of the Indian Patents and Designs Act. The current governing legislation is the Patents Act of 1970, which took effect in 1972. The oversight of

the Indian Patent Act falls under the responsibility of the Office of the Controller General of Patents, Designs, and Trade Marks (CGPDTM). The Patent Office has its primary location in Calcutta, along with branches in New Delhi, Chennai, and Mumbai. The CGPDTM office is situated in Mumbai, while Nagpur houses the Patent Information System office and the National Institute for Intellectual Property Management.

- The Controller General plays a pivotal role in administering the Act and provides advisory assistance to the government on related matters. Amendments to the Patents Act were implemented in 1999, 2002, 2005, and 2006 to align with the Trade-Related Aspects of Intellectual Property Rights (TRIPS). A significant amendment occurred in 2005, extending product patents to all technological fields, encompassing food, drugs, chemicals, and microorganisms. Subsequent amendments to the Rules under the Patent Act were carried out in 2012, 2013, and 2014.
- The certain conditions required for patentability are Novelty, non-obviousness, usefulness, and industrial applicability.

Intellectual Property Rights

- Intellectual Property (IP) rights entail granting property rights through patents, copyrights, and trademarks. Individuals or entities with intellectual property rights have exclusive control over the utilization of specific property or items for a specified duration.
- The term "intellectual property" was introduced in the 19th century, gaining widespread incorporation into legal systems globally during the 20th century. There are 4 main types of intellectual property rights; patents, copyrights, trademarks, trade secrets.

Emergency Use Authorization (EUA)

- The Emergency Use Authorization (EUA) authority empowers the FDA to enhance the nation's public health defenses against chemical, biological, radiological, and nuclear (CBRN) threats, encompassing infectious diseases. This is achieved by streamlining the availability and usage of medical countermeasures (MCMs) essential during public health emergencies.
- Under the EUA, the FDA has the ability to grant authorization for the use of either an unapproved medical product or the employment of an approved medical product for an unapproved purpose in emergency situations. Such authorization is given when the FDA determines that the benefits of the product outweigh its known and potential risks, and there are no adequate, approved, and available alternatives for the intended use.

- EUA can be applied to various medical products, including drugs, vaccines, diagnostic tests, and more. Particularly during the COVID-19 pandemic, the EUA has been extensively utilized to expedite the development and dissemination of COVID-19 vaccines, treatments, and diagnostic tests.

CHAPTER 15

Blood Bank

Introduction

In the year 1998 there were reports of maternal mortality ratio with an estimated 407 deaths per 100,000 population to reduce this estimate to 100 by the year 2010 National Population Policy 2000 took the initiative to do so. Most of the maternal mortalities were during pregnancy and childbirth due to postpartum haemorrhage, Obstructed labour, anaemia, Unsafe termination of pregnancies, and hypertensive disorders. Haemorrhages during pregnancy are unpredictable so the availability of emergency obstetric care services and timely action becomes vital to handle these sensitive cases. so, under the CSSM Programme (1992-1997) various first referral units were set up at various community health centres and were provided with equipment kits of 12 different types which were labelled as necessary for caesarean sections and other surgical interventions related to maternal health care. However, there was still a lack of blood transfusion facilities in these units which was a hurdle to the proper working of these units. to overcome this hurdle of FRU the Drug and Cosmetics Act was amended with the objective of including blood storage facilities at FRUs to support maternal delivery emergencies. this notification included the aim of providing sufficient high-quality human blood and its components at hospitals with licenses and those without licenses including only those hospitals that perform blood transfusions of less than 2000 units/year. Along with this, there were some notifications issued under Annexure 1 by the Ministry of Health and Family Welfare. To support this initiative, the Department of family welfare under the government of India promised to provide equipment and training of staff for blood transfusion facilities in FRU's even in those hospitals where the facility is not a part of NACO and the National AIDS Control Organisation provided different types of blood storage refrigerators to various states. within this chapter, there will be a discussion related to various guidelines related to blood bank setup along with their basic functions and requirements.

In the modern health care system, blood transfusion services (BTS) are an essential component without which emergency treatment is not possible. the provision of safe blood and blood products is the responsibility of governmental health authorities with continuous efforts there has been increased safe blood availability from 4.4 million units in 2007 to 10.8 million units in 2016 along with an increase in voluntary donation of blood also there was reported to be a decrease in the HIV sero-reactivity from 1.2-0.12% as per the data of NACO, 2013.

Even after all this, there are still various challenges associated with the delivery of safe blood and blood products major of which are related to blood banks. In blood banks, there is a lack of trained human resources and quality management systems for blood products. The National Blood Policy, 2002 has mentioned in Objective 6

Objective

The objective of educating and training human resources under human resource development. according to this objective, there is a need to encourage the posting of doctors for at least 18 days in blood banks under the compulsory rotational internship and the postgraduate and diploma courses in transfusion medicine should also be included in different health-related courses. as per the central drugs standard control organization, India's National Blood Policy, 2002 Blood bank is defined as facilities which are licensed for the collection, storage, processing, testing, separation, and distribution of human blood and its components.

Various Services Provided in a Blood Bank

Collection of blood from donors which may include Apheresis and Autologous blood, in the former there is a donation of plasma or platelets, and the remaining blood elements are transfused back to the donor during blood collection. The latter includes the collection of blood from a patient to transfuse into the same donor at a later date.

- Storage of blood.
- Grouping of blood and testing for compatibility.
- Testing of blood for communicable diseases like HIV.

Approval of blood storage facilities

The approval of these facilities are obtained from state or union territories licensing authorities by filing an application compiled by following guidelines in annexure 1. once the conditions and facilities are inspected to be approving the basic guidelines the blood storage unit is provided with the approval from the authorised officials. This approval lats for 2 years unless it is suspended before the date of expiry and to renew this approval another renewal application needs to be submitted 3 months before the date of expiry.

Collection and processing of blood

There are several types of blood which is transfused like whole blood, transfusion of Platelet and transfusion of Plasma. Whole blood is defined as transfusion of blood without separation. Patients with anaemia are transfused with red blood cells which are used to improve oxygen saturation of body, these red blood cells can be stored for 35-45 days at 2-6°C.as for platelet transfusion the platelets are transfused from patients with high platelet count to patients which are deficient in platelets, which is expensive due to isolation of platelets. The platelets can be stored for up to 5-7 days at room temperature. plasma transfusion involves the isolation of plasma from the donor's blood known as plasmapheresis which can be stored up to 12 months at a temperature of -30°C. Within the U.S. certain standards have been set for blood and its products. Whole blood is defined as venous blood which is unseparated and an approved preservative is added to this in order to maintain its shelf life. In order to separate components of whole blood with RBC the whole blood is centrifuged. Whole blood and RBC units are stored for a period of 35-42 days at a temperature of 33.8-42.8°F. Units of RBC are frozen in glycerol which is rather expensive and rarely done. These frozen RBC units are stored at -85°F for a period of 10 years. The less dense plasma from blood is used for various frozen components manufacturing. based on whether the plasma was frozen and will be used for transfusion it is labelled as fresh frozen plasma and when plasma is used for production of other components (e.g. cryoprecipitate) it is known as fractionation of plasma.

Testing of blood

The blood donors are tested for various disease markers to prevent transmission of infectious disease via blood or blood components to the receptor population and prevent any life fatality. The various tests conducted includes: screening for parasite called Trypanosoma cruzi (anti-T.cruzi) usinf ELISA(Enzyme Linked Immunosorbent Assay) and ESA(Enzyme Strip Immunoassay) which is known to cause Chagas disease, Hepatitis B Virus(HBV DNA, HBsAg, Anti-HBc) using Genetic Systems distributed by ortho(GS), HBsAg EIA 3.0 ,ELISA qualitative analysis for detection of HBsAg, Ortho HBc ELISA for detection of HBV core antigen(anti-HBc) antibodies, Screening of Hepatitis C virus using Ortho HCV ELISA , Duplex NAT, Screening of Human Immunodeficiency viruses (type 1 and 2) using Genetic Systems distributed by ortho(GS), HIV-1/HIV-2 PLUS O EIA, Duplex NAT, screening of Human T-Lymphotropic Virus(HTLV-1 and 2) using Avioq HTLV-1/2 Micrelisa system, western blotting, screening of Syphilis using EIA, testing of antibodies against Spirochete, screening of Zika virus(ZIKV) associated with dengue viruses using NAT(Nucleic Acid Test), screening of West Nile Virus(WNV) using NAT (Nucleic acid testing), screening of Babesia antibody against Babesia a red cell parasite causing babesiosis using NAT assay , IFA(Indirect Immunofluorescence assay) for assay of antibodies.. their tests includes Cytomegalovirus antibody testing , and Human Leukocyte Antigens(HLA) antibody testing. (3)

Storage and Management

As per guidelines from central government Blood cold chain system needs to be followed in order to prevent any danger to blood recipient. Blood Cold Chain is defined as a systemic process of keeping the blood at correct temperature from collection of blood till administration of blood to the recipient while transporting and storing the blood and blood components safely. The various equipment used for the storage of blood includes Plasma freezers, Platelet agitator cum incubators, Blood bank refrigerators, and blood transport boxes.

Legal Framework Scenario

Human blood is covered under section 3(b) in the drug definition of the Drugs and cosmetics act. so, the regulation of blood banks is of vital importance. In year 1967 ministry of health, the central government covered requirements for accommodation, technical staff and equipment vital for working of blood banks in schedule F Part XII B under drugs and cosmetic act. The Indian pharmacopeia is set as standard for whole human blood.

Another notification issued by ministry of health and family welfare in year 1989 made the testing for HIV 1 and 2 antibodies in whole blood. in year 1990 each unit of blood was regulated and three main laboratories like NICD Delhi, NIV Pune and CMC, Vellore were notified to work according to 3A guidelines for laboratories for testing of HIV antibodies in human blood and products. In year 1992-93 the drug and cosmetic rules 68A, Part XB and Part XIIB of schedule F were amended after noticing deficiencies in quality control of blood and its products. The power was handed to drug controller general of India regarding power of central license approving authority (CLAA) for blood and products like IV fluids and sera.

Part X-B of D&C rules from 122F-122P cover the procedure for applications by blood banks, fees requirement for grant and renewal of license and various conditions followed by applicant after grant and renewal. as per supreme court order legislation for blood banks were revised on 5th April 1999 to incorporate GMP, SOP and validation of equipment.

Requirements for Grant and Renewal of Blood Bank Licenses

122-EA

Definitions: various definitions are covered under schedule A in part XIIB and Part XIIC of Schedule F are

Autologous blood defined as blood transfused for re transfusion into the same individuals later on.

Apheresis defines process by which blood is drawn from donor and after separation from plasma and platelets is re transfused into another donor simultaneously.

Blood bank is a place/organization/ unit/institution for carrying out collection, apheresis, storage, processing and distribution of blood from donors and preparation and storage of these blood components.

Blood components is defined as drug prepared, obtained, derived and separated from drawn flood from a donor.

Blood product is defined as a drug manufactured from pooled plasma by fractionation

A donor is defined as a person who voluntarily donates blood after being declared fit without any cash or any other kind of consideration like medals, time off work, certificates, blood assurance program membership, gifts, etc.

Leucapheresis is a process through which blood is drawn from a donor after the separation of leucocyte concentrations which is transfused back into the said donor.

Plateletpheresis is a process by which blood is drawn from the donor and is re transfused into said donor after separation from platelet.

Plasmapheresis is process by which the drawn blood is separated from plasma for re transfusion into said donor.

Professional donor is a person who donates blood for cash or other kind of consideration from any source on behalf of recipient patient and includes a commercial donor.

Replacement donor is a person who is family friend and relative of patient donating blood to said donor.

122F

Application form for licence for blood bank operation and processing of whole human blood for components, manufacture, sale and distribution.

1. Application for purpose of grant/renewal of license for operation of blood bank and processing of human blood for components and manufacture of blood products. The submission of this application is accompanied by license fees of 6,000 rupees and inspection fee of 1500 rupees/ inspection for renewal of license. This granting and renewal is granted by licensing authority under part VII in Form 27-C/Form 27-E. when the applicant applies for renewal within 6 months from expiry of license then in addition to inspection fee of 1500 and license fee of 6000 rupees additional fees of 1,000/month delayed needs to be paid.

2. In case the original license is damaged, defaced or lost, the copy of license can be issued at fee of 1,000 rupees for duplicate copy.
3. Each drug mentioned in the application is accompanied by 300 rupees.
4. The licensing authority shall mention following things on receipt for application of front and renewal of license like statement verification in application form, manufacturing cause and establishment testing inspected as per provisions of rules 122-I, for renewal application of license past information of license should be mentioned.
5. After making sure if licensee is in position to fulfil the requirement of the licensing authority, the said authority prepares a report which is forwarded along with application for grant of license in triplicate to the central license approving authority. however, if the authority considers the licensee to not meet the requirement for granting the license, then the reason is recorded in writing along with refusal of grant or renewal of license.
6. Only after report by licensing authority under subrule 5 and inspection by inspectors under section 21 the central license approving authority considers the requirements to be fulfilled and grants/renews license.

122G

The form for license for operation and working of whole blood processing for components and blood products manufacture and license renewal or grant. The license for operation and processing of whole human blood components and blood products manufacture is issued under form 28-C/26G/Form 26-I. Before granting and renewal of license following conditions need to be met by licensee:

1. The processing and manufacture of whole human blood components and products should be done in active supervision of component technical staff (medical officer. Either have a post graduate degree in medicine/ Degree in medicine with diploma in pathology or transfusion medicines/Degree in medicine having experience of 1 year in blood bank during regular service).
2. The space requirement for plant and equipment for collection and processing of blood should be met as given in schedule F, Part XII-B/XII-C.
3. The technical staff should be maintained as per schedule F, Part XII-B/XII-C.
4. Arrangements for storage of whole human blood, components and products should be made available by the applicant.
5. The data regarding stability and shelf life of products should be made available to licensing authority.

122-H

Duration of license: the original license in form 28-C/28-E and renewed license under form 26-G/26-I is valid for a period of 5 years and from the same date of the same year on which it was granted.

122-I

Inspection before grant/renewal of license for blood bank operation and processing of Whole human blood for components and products: before approval the inspectors inspect every part of the premises, working of equipment and various components of blood being manufactured and processed along with their processes.

122-J

Inspector report: the inspectors forward a detailed descriptive report including its findings and recommendations.

122-K

Application after rejection: if within 6 months of rejection the applicant informs the licensing authority about the requirements being satisfied and deposits inspection fee of 250 rupees to licensing authority then after inspection if the authority is satisfied then it shall grant or renew the license under form 28-C/28-E.

122-L

Power delegation by central licensing authority: the controlling authority must meet the requirements mentioned under rule 50-A and they have the power to sign the licenses.

122-M

Appeal provision to state government by licensee whose license has not been granted/renewed: within 30 days from rejection order receipt, the licensee can apply for enquiry to state government/central government.

122-N

Additional information that needs to be provided b the license to the licensing authority: documentary evidence for ownership/rental/other basis, specification in application for license, firm constitution required for verification purposes of statement correctness by licensee.

122-O

Cancellation and license suspension: during inspection if the authority considers the requirement to not be met then he shall pass the order for cancellation of license. The license will be cancelled and suspended within 3 months from date of order under subrule 1.

122-P

License conditions: the license in form 28-C, 28-E, 26-G, 26-I should be subjected to special conditions mentioned in schedule Part XII-B.XII-C which is related to substance for which license is being granted/renewed.

CHAPTER 16

Clinical Establishment Act and Rules

Introduction

The Registration and Regulation of Clinical Establishments Act,2010 was approved by the central government to provide registration and regulation for all clinical establishments across the country with the aim of prescribing minimum standards to facilities and services provided by these establishments. This act was enacted in 2010 by the central government and has since been adopted by some states and union territories. The act took effect on 1st March 2012 in four states: Arunachal Pradesh, Mizoram, Himachal Pradesh, Sikkim, and all union territories excluding the NCT of Delhi. Other states like Rajasthan, Bihar, Uttar Pradesh, Jharkhand, Assam, Haryana, and Uttarakhand adopted this act under clause (1) of article 252 of the Indian constitution. The rules under clinical establishment rules are a government-issued set of regulations and guidelines for the regulation of clinical establishments within the country. Various clinical establishments covered under this act are single-doctor clinics. It also provides information on registration procedure, renewal, inspection, cancellation, and penalty. Another aim of this act is to improve the overall quality and accountability of health services across the country and to improve public health, article 47 needs to be mandated.

Rules

THE CLINICAL ESTABLISHMENTS (REGISTRATION AND REGULATION) ACT, 2010: considered the primary regulation governing clinical establishments within the country. Compiles guidelines for registration and regulation of clinical facilities like clinics, diagnostic centres, and hospitals, maintenance of standards for these establishments and services, inspection and mechanism of monitoring, grievance redressal system, and non-compliance penalties. Some clinical establishment rules notified by central government or state governments include the Clinical Establishments (central government) rules,2012, the Clinical Establishments (registration and regulation) Haryana government rules, 2014, the Clinical Establishments (registration and regulation) Rajasthan Rules, 2011, the clinical establishments (registration and regulation) Uttar Pradesh rules, 2018, the clinical establishments(registration and regulation) Uttarakhand rules, 2016, the clinical establishments (registration and regulation) Bihar rules, 2013, the clinical establishments(registration and regulation) Jharkhand rules, 2015 and the clinical establishments(registration and regulation) Assam rules, 2018.

Minimum Standards of Medical Education and Training Regulations,2020

These regulations compile the minimum standards of medical education and training in India along with the specification of criteria for recognition in medical colleges and institutions. governing quality and medical education content along with training in different countries and regions is a vital part of these regulations. The major aim includes ensuring standard setting to produce competent, ethical, and knowledgeable in the latest scientific and clinical developments in medical graduates and professionals in their respective fields. In India, the National Medical Commission (NMC) is the regulatory body for issuing regulations for medical education and training. The regulations issued include post-graduate medical education regulations-2023, the minimum standard of requirements for postgraduate courses-2023 which defines objectives, curriculum, outcomes, faculty, infrastructure, and assessment criteria for postgraduate medical courses. For a similar purpose UK regulatory body called the General Medical Council (GMC) is a medical education regulator and practice regulator whereas the Union Européenne des Médecins Spécialistes (UEMS) is the representative medical organization for Europe.

National Accreditation Board for Hospitals and Healthcare Providers (NABH) Standards

The Quality Council of India has a constituent board of NABH which in conjunction with consultation with stakeholders developed standards to provide a framework for quality and safety assessment of healthcare services in India. The standards under NABH define health care quality and safety provided by accredited organizations. The provided standards are based on international benchmarks which are revised periodically in response to the latest developments in the healthcare sector. The various aspects include human resources, clinical care, patient rights, education, infection control, quality control, and governance. The main aim covered by NABH standards is to provide safe, effective, and ethical healthcare to patients by enhancing the credibility and reputation of healthcare organizations, and maintain continuous quality improvement.

Indian Medical Council (Professional Conduct, Etiquette, and Ethics) Regulations, 2002

These regulations compile a code of conduct, etiquette, and ethics for medical practitioners setting guidelines for patient care, confidentiality, and professional care. These regulations were issued by MCI (Medical Council of India) under the Indian Medical Council Act,1956 after central government approval. Various aspects covered are physician character and duties, patient rights and responsibilities, physician relationship with other physicians, and public and paramedical staff. Medical services fees, maintenance of medical records, confidentiality, ethical issues, disciplinary action, and penalties against misconduct and violation of regulations.

Consumer Protection Act, 2019

This act includes comprehensive law responsible for protecting the rights of customers in India and includes the consumer courts establishments and consumer grievances redressal including those related to healthcare services as well. This act came into force in the year 2020 after replacing the Consumer Protection Act, of 1986. Some salient features of this act include promoting investigations, recalling unsafe goods and services, and imposing penalties for false advertisements via the Central Consumer Protection Authority (CCPA). Empowers Consumer Disputes Redressal Commissions (CDRCs) at national/district/state levels to handle defect complaints in goods and services, unfair contracts, e-commerce transactions, and overcharging. Besides this, it also facilitates complaint filing using electrical means and performs hearing through virtual means. Also, it safeguards consumer rights like the right to information, right to choose, right to safety, right to redress, and right to consumer education. This act is also stated as responsible for introducing product liability making manufacturers/sellers/service providers for compensation of any harm to consumers for defective products/services.

Drugs and Cosmetics Act,1940

Responsible for regulating import, manufacture, and drugs and cosmetics sales in India by setting standards for the quality, safety, and efficacy of these products. Main aspects covered under this act are providing penalties for violating rules under this act and setting rules and regulations for the implementation of provisions to prohibit the import, manufacture, and sale of drugs or cosmetics. This act also prohibits the manufacture/sale and import of misbranded, adulterated, and spurious drugs and empowers the central drugs laboratory and the drugs consultative committee for assistance on technical and scientific matters on drugs/cosmetics.

Indian Nursing Council Act, 1947

This law is aimed at establishing training standards for midwives, nurses, and health visitors in India which regulates the regulations, education, and professional conduct of health service providers. Indian Nursing Council is a body that advises and assists the government on matters related to government. The provisions under this act include defining qualifications and conditions of nurses, midwives, and health visitors' enrollment in state registers, empowering the council for prescription of syllabus, curriculum, and examinations for nursing courses and recognitions in various institutions. This act is also responsible for inspecting and supervising state council functioning and takes disciplinary action against any misconduct related to the nursing field along with issuing certificates and badges to registered medical practitioners.

The Clinical Establishment Act, of 2010 is a law to set regulations and registration for all clinical establishments in India while also prescribing minimum standards for the safety and quality of health care in these establishments.

Some salient features of this act are: providing advice to the government related to clinical establishments and obtaining provisional registration certificates from state government authorities. Under this act, inspectors are empowered to inspect, monitor, and cancellation of clinical establishment registration after violation of provided guidelines. sets certain rules and regulations that pharmacies must follow to ensure the safety and well-being of parents.

Registration

The clinical establishments must be registered with regulatory authorities and during the regulatory process information on ownership, infrastructure, location, and services offered must be submitted by the pharmacy. Some of the common requirements for registration of medical practitioners are Completing an accredited medical degree or equivalent qualification from a recognized institution. Passing a national or state-level licensing exam or assessment that tests the knowledge, skills, and competence of the practitioner. Applying for registration with the relevant medical authority or board that regulates the profession in the country or state of practice. Meeting the standards of professional conduct, ethics, and continuing education as prescribed by the medical authority or board. Paying the registration fees and renewing the registration periodically.

Qualification and training

Pharmacists working in clinical establishments must have some qualifications and training appropriate for the field of work as per guidelines of the Pharmacy Council of India. The registration of pharmacists needs to be renewed every 5 years and must involve regular training to stay up-to-date about newer developments in the pharmacy field.

Quality of Drugs and Services

The quality of drugs and services offered to individuals must be as per standards which include proper storage of drugs, checking expiry status of drugs, and maintaining proper records of drugs related to invoices and other details.

Patient safety

The legibility and accuracy of prescription safety needs to be done along with maintenance of confidentiality, and provision of adequate information regarding drug use. The safety of patients can be ensured after the prevention of errors and Adverse effects related to treatment, diagnosis, and follow-up care. Common sources of patient harm are prescription errors, diagnosis errors, pressure ulcers, patient falls, and surgical errors along with many more reasons.

CHAPTER 17

Biomedical Waste Management Rules 2016

Introduction

Biomedical waste can be defined as any kind of waste which is generated during diagnosis, treatment, or immunization of humans or animals or during research activities. The waste generated during production or testing of biological products also constituted biomedical waste. Biomedical waste comprises of human & animal anatomical waste, needles, syringes, and other materials that are used in health care facilities during treatment and research.

The biomedical waste management rules 2016 can be defined as a set of regulations that provide guidance on the safe handling, segregation, transportation, and disposal of biomedical waste. These rules are applicable to all persons who generate, collect, store, transport, treat, dispose of or handle biomedical waste in any form.

Basic Aspects of Biomedical Waste Management Rules 2016 (BMWM)

According to Biomedical waste management rules, on the basis of segregation pathway and color code the waste generated is classified under 4 categories, these are Yellow category, Red category, White category, and Blue category

1. **Yellow category:** Human and Animal Anatomical Waste like human tissues, body parts, waste generated from animals which are used in experiments are included under yellow category. Certain items which are contaminated by blood, body fluids, cotton swabs, expired medicines or drugs which are cytotoxic, discarded disinfectants also comes under this category. The liquid waste from laboratories and floor washing, discarded formalin and use of silver –X ray film developing liquid are all examples of chemical liquid waste which are included under the yellow category. Further the waste generated from microbiological labs, biotechnological labs or any other clinical laboratories are placed under yellow category.

2. **Red category:** Waste produced from single-use items, including tubing, bottles, intravenous tubes and sets, catheters, urine bags, syringes without needles, fixed needle syringes with their needles removed, and gloves
3. **White category:** this includes those items which are sharp like needles, syringes, blades or any other contaminated sharp object that may cause puncture and cuts.
4. **Blue category:** includes the broken or contaminated glasses like that of vials, and ampoules except those which contain any cytotoxic waste.

Salient Features of Biomedical Waste Management Rules 2016

1. The regulations now include a wider range of health camps, including blood donation, immunization, and surgery camps.
2. Occupier is an individual having administrative control over the Health Care Facility that is generating BMW. Duties related to occupier have been revised.
3. The pretreatment of waste by method of sterilization and disinfectant shall be in accordance with WHO. Gradually stopping the use of chlorinated plastic bags, and gloves.
4. Liquid waste should undergo source separation through pretreatment before being combined with other liquid waste.
5. Daily maintenance of biomedical waste management disposal register and to be updated monthly on website.
6. Emission standards for incinerators have been updated to adhere to environmentally friendly practices.

Steps Involved in Bio-Medical Waste Management

There are 5 steps which are involved in biomedical waste management these 5 steps are Segregation, Collection, pre-treatment, Intramural Transportation and Storage.

1. **Bio Medical Waste Segregation:** Segregation of waste must be started at point of generation only. The point of origin is where waste is initially generated, accumulates, and falls under the supervision of medical personnel, including doctors or nursing staff, who are administering treatment to patients and, consequently, producing biomedical waste. Color coded bins to be present and waste material to be segregated properly in those bins.
2. **Collection:** The time of collection shall be fixed and be performed daily. Those collecting biomedical waste shall wear personal protective equipment. The collection of biomedical waste should not be collected in the same trolley which is used for collection of general waste. All bags, containers, or bins used for the collection and storage of biomedical waste

must be labeled accordingly with either the Biohazard Symbol or Cytotoxic Hazard Symbol, depending on the type of waste, following the guidelines outlined in the BMWM Rules, 2016.

3. **Storage:** Leak proof and puncture-resistant container shall be used for storage of biomedical waste. The container should contain a proper label and should be closed properly. Separate area should be prepared for storing of container away from patient care area.
4. **Transportation:** after collection of waste it is transported to a specific area. During transportation of waste it should follow a path that involves less number of person coming in contact. Safe transportation of waste is undertaken to avoid spillage and scattering of waste.
5. **Pre-treatment:** Biomedical waste should be properly treated and then disposed of in surroundings, such that it is eco-friendly with the nature. There are varieties of treatment methods available like incineration, microwave treatment, chemical disinfection, any of the method can be opted for treating biomedical waste. Treatment option for yellow category waste is incineration, for red category is sterilization and then recycling, for white category is dry heat sterilization and for blue category treatment option is disinfection and then recycling.

Aspects Related to Pharma Manufacture to Disposal of Pharma/ Medical Waste at

Homes

Biomedical waste is not only generated by the hospitals, pharmacies but also generated by homes. Like the use of needles, syringe, and expired medications present in house constitute a biomedical waste. So houses should also follow a specific method for disposal of biomedical waste. Returning of expired medications to pharmacies for their disposal and storing of sharp objects like needles in puncture resistant containers and then discarding them are certain steps that shall be taken at household level. The clear instructions on how to store and dispose of the waste should be provided to the patients.

Pharmacies

Pharmaceutical manufacturing facilities generate a significant amount of biomedical waste. Pharmaceutical waste comprises expired medications, patients' unused personal drugs, syringes, IV bags, tubing, vials, and materials containing residues of chemotherapy drugs. It also includes open containers of drugs that are unusable and containers holding acute hazardous waste drugs. Pharmaceutical waste can be classified into Hazardous waste, Non-hazardous waste, and Chemo waste. Disposal of pharma waste includes certain steps, first step being Segregation of Pharmaceutical waste from other biomedical waste and to storing in desired containers for further treatment. Second step being Disposal of waste, there are various methods for disposal of pharmaceutical waste like incineration, recyclers, autoclaving, microwaving, chemical disinfection, deep burial, waste immobilization and secure land filling. Third step is reverse logistics which is used for collection and disposal of unused and expired medicines.

(i) **Incinerations:** In this process solid organic waste is subjected to combustion in order to reduce amount of waste. This method is suitable for both solid waste management and solid residue from waste water management. It is also referred to as thermal treatment due to high temperature used to convert waste into residue and certain gases are also produced during this process.

(ii) **Autoclaving:** is used in order to kill pathogens present on biomedical waste. A saturated steam kills the pathogen by coming in direct contact with it for certain time and at specific temperature. The waste produced through autoclaving can be disposed of in landfills together with other municipal waste.

(iii) **Microwaving:** Before microwaving waste should be reduced to specific size. Upon application of electromagnetic field on biomedical waste, the liquid present in the waste starts oscillating and eventually gets heated up thereby killing the infectious component.

(iv) **Chemical disinfection:** The disinfection efficiency of disinfectant depends upon type and amount of chemical used. This method is used for treating liquid waste such as blood, urine, stools, or health care facility sewage.

(v) **Deep burial:** In this process all the biomedical waste is placed in the pit. Pit is covered half with waste first and then covered with lime before filling rest of pit with soil.

(vi) **Secure land filling:** The regulations outlined in the Biomedical Waste Rules stipulate that unused medicines, cytotoxic drugs, solid chemical wastes, and incineration ash must be disposed of in specifically designated secure landfills. However a landfill causes a number of adverse environmental impacts such as attraction of vermin, and generation of liquid leachate.

(vii) **Waste immobilization:** Encapsulation and Inertization are two types of techniques included in the waste immobilization. The encapsulation is the process of immobilizing the pharmaceutical waste by placing it in the plastic or steel drum. The drums used for holding waste should be cleaned and should hold only 75% of the solid waste material. After filling 75% with waste the mixture of lime, cement and water in the proportions 15:15:5 (by weight) is added. Inertization involves removing the packaging materials, paper, cardboard and plastic, from the pharmaceuticals. The pharmaceuticals are then ground and a mix of water, cement and lime added to form a homogenous paste. The so formed paste is decanted into the normal urban waste which sets as solid mass with municipal waste.

Hospitals

Hospitals also generate a large volume of biomedical waste like sharps, infectious waste and anatomical waste. Similar steps as discussed above are followed for disposing of waste generated in hospitals.

- Healthcare workers working in pharmacies and hospitals are required to undergo training on biomedical waste management regarding segregation, handling, and disposal practices.
- The maintenance of records related to the generation, collection, reception, storage, transportation, treatment, and disposal is obligatory in accordance with the rules for duration of five years.
- No untreated bio-medical waste shall be kept stored beyond a period of 48 hours.
- Treatment and disposal of biomedical waste should be eco-friendly.
- Authorized personnel only after wearing personnel protective equipment's shall collect and treat the waste.

Hazardous Waste Management Strategy

There are 3 different methods of managing waste these are waste minimization, reuse and recycling. Prevention of generation of waste is the best method to reduce waste; it includes using secondhand products, repairing broken items instead of buying new. Reuse avoids discarding a material to a waste stream when its initial use has concluded. Recycling benefits the environment by reducing the use of virgin materials.

CHAPTER 18

Bioethics

Introduction

Earlier there was no kind of regulation posed for research activity on humans but after the Second World War, research activities were highly regulated. Firstly, Nuremberg code was formulated in 1947. In 1948, universal declaration of human rights expressed concern about rights of human beings being subjected to involuntary maltreatment. Many rules came and are still followed in order to protect and safeguard the rights of individuals.

Ethics are moral principles to be followed by an individual in day to day life. Similarly medical ethics is the branch of ethics that focuses on how to deal with the moral issues arising in the field of medical practices. Bioethics on other hand is a broad term that includes medical ethics and focuses on issues related to health care, in conduct of research and various other research related issues. One can clearly define bioethics as, the branch that examines the ethical, social, and legal implications of biomedical research. It specifically deals with the questions what is right or wrong in healthcare along with this provides ethical guidance to researchers, and healthcare professionals.

Basic Concept of Bioethics

- In the field of medicine many times it have been seen that a dilemma may arise concerned with patient autonomy, beneficence, non-maleficence, justice, and the sanctity of life. In order to resolve this dilemma and to overcome such kind of situation in future bioethics are referred.
- Bioethics combines both scientific and humanistic components. It states that feelings of patients based on personal, social, cultural and economic values are respected and physician shall work according to the best interest of patients.

History of Bioethics

- Late in the year 1960 and 1970s bioethics emerged as unique field in order to solve the high raising controversies in the area of medicine and biomedical practices.

- Back in the history there have been many controversies, one such controversies was of Tuskegee syphilis study in which man who was suffering from syphilis was left untreated in order to study how the disease negatively affects the ones performing abilities.
- Despite the results produced by this study it was highly criticized. It was criticized due to its unethical practices i.e. leaving a man in diseased condition without providing him a necessary treatment for the sake of research.
- After this study a report was issued called Belmont Report, this Belmont report necessitates the establishment of ethical principles of respect for person, beneficence, justice and non-maleficence.

Principle of Bioethics

There are basically 4 principles of bioethics which are based upon ethical considerations which arise in practice of medicine and biomedical research. These principles include autonomy, beneficence, non-maleficence and justice. Dignity, truthfulness and honesty are certain other principles that are to be followed.

1. **Autonomy:** This principle states that patient has the right to either refuse or accept the treatment and no undue influence can change his mind or force to undergo a specific treatment. Physicians at all times should respect the autonomy of patients.
2. **Beneficence:** This principle states that the physicians shall act according to best interest of patients. However it has been seen that sometimes physicians for their own self-interest violate the principle of beneficence.
3. **Non-Maleficence:** This principle states that physician shall not cause any harm to the patients and should always take precautions to prevent any harm to patients.
4. **Justice:** Health treatment options shall be equally distributed to all patients irrespective of their economic status. This principle deals with distribution of scarce health resources equally among all.
5. **Dignity:** This principle state that patients are respected for the choice of treatment option they opt for and patients are always treated with dignity and respect.
6. **Truthfulness and honesty:** Before undergoing any research activity it is mandatory to sign an informed consent process. The informed consent provides that patients know which kind of research they are undergoing and have given their consent after complete understanding and at no stage they will be used for any other activity which is not mentioned previously.

Conflict of Principles

A conflict may arise when primary interest of physician is influenced by a secondary interest like financial gain or prestige. However physician shall avoid these conflicts and should give their best. Conflict can be between autonomy and Beneficence or between autonomy and non-maleficence. Whenever patients disagree with a particular kind of treatment option as suggested by physician, then a conflict occurs. This represents the conflict between autonomy and beneficence. Sometimes autonomy and beneficence may overlap like when patients autonomy is breached this kind of situation decreases confidence for medical services and this causes inability to perform beneficence.

Indian Council of Medical Research (ICMR)

ICMR has developed the, "National Ethical Guidelines for Biomedical and Health Research

Involving Human Participants". These guidelines provide guidance on how to ethically conduct biomedical and health research involving human participants. This guideline provides guidance on various issues in research that includes informed consent, confidentiality, risk assessment, and the use of vulnerable populations. The guidance is provided to all those who are involved in research whether be the researcher or other stakeholders.

General principles

As per the guidelines there are different principles which are to be followed, these principles are:

- **Principles of essentiality:** This principle states that use of human participants is considered essential for the research only after considering all alternatives and should be approved by ethical committee.
- **Principle of voluntariness:** According to this, principle the right of participants is given first preference. The right of participant either to continue the study or to withdraw from study is respected and is not influenced to go against their wish.
- **Principles of non-exploitation:** This deals with selection of participants so that both risk and benefit are equally distributed between the participants without any discrimination and ensures safeguards for protecting vulnerable groups.
- **Principles of privacy and confidentiality:** The records of patients are kept under privacy and only authorized persons can have access to the data. However under certain circumstances the privacy can be breached but only after consultation from the Ethical committee.

- **Principles of professional competence:** This states that the research can be conducted only by the persons who are having a particular qualification, training and experience.
- **Principles of precaution and risk minimization:** Research should ensure minimum risk to the participants, if any risk has caused harm to the participants then they should be compensated for the same.
- **Principles of accountability and transparency:** Whatever outcome is derived from the research it is to be presented to the public through registries, reports without breaching the privacy of participants.
- **Principles of the maximization of benefit:** The research is always planned in such a way that minimum risk and maximum benefits are produced.
- **Principles of institutional arrangements:** The institutions where research is to be performed have proper policies for governing the research and should provide all the required infrastructure, training to conduct the research.

General ethical issues

It is the duty of the researcher to protect the rights of an individual and to conduct the research based on the above principles. The researchers before conducting the research should ascertain the risk and benefit ratio and can be carried on humans only when benefits overweight than risk.

- Ethical committee should review the research process to look for any risk associated if the high risk is associated then either research is discontinued or certain alterations are made in order to reduce risk. Also, all the type of expenses that a participant undergoes like travel expenses shall be reimbursed. It is the duty of ethical committee to ensure that no undue inducements are involved in payment and should approve the payments after complete review only.
- Further compensation is to be provided in case of any harm or inconvenience to participants occurs during research. There should be standard operating procedures in order to mitigate and manage conflict of interest even between ethical committee.
- For conducting the research vulnerable groups are usually avoided and included only when the study deals with effect on these participants only. Both the children and person suffering from clinical conditions like cognitive impairment, unconsciousness etc. are included in vulnerable groups.
- Study protocol should clearly mention the plans for sharing of post research activities and results. Results derived from the research should be communicated to the community for their benefit.

Responsible conduct of research

The values, policies, planning and conducting research, reviewing and reporting research, and responsible authorship and publication are all included under responsible conduct of research (RCR).

- **Values of research:** Honesty, accuracy, efficiency, fairness, objectivity, reliability and accountability are certain values that are required to be followed for conducting research.
- **Policies:** All the policies regarding monitoring of research, data capture, reporting of scientific misconduct and conflict of interest shall be present on the websites of institutions.
- **Reviewing and reporting research:** Whenever research is completed it needs to be published irrespective of its results so that no other participants undergo the same process to obtain same results.
- **Research misconduct and policies for handling misconduct:** In case of any kind of misconduct, institutions shall have procedures to investigate, mitigate them and to take proper action against the accused person.

Ethics Committee Review

Ethical committees are multi-disciplinary and multi-sectoral in nature. Ethical committees have around 7 to 15 members and to meet the quorum requirements minimum number of 5 members must be present. All the decision regarding approval or discontinue of research projects are to be made by ethical committee after reviewing all aspects properly.

1. **Informed Consent process:** Human participants are free to choose whether they want to continue the research or the not. Informed consent provides the information about the research aim and objective to the participants and ensures that they know all the risk and benefits associated with the disease. Individuals can participate in research after filling informed consent, in case individual is not capable to fill form, then any other person on behalf of him can fill the form and participate in the research.
2. **Confidentiality and Privacy:** When picking sensitive study areas, particular contexts, and settings, as well as data collection sites, it is important to take research participants' privacy and confidentiality into account. Under some conditions, study volunteers may become more susceptible due to increased hazards in terms of psychology, society, health, or law. Participants in these studies who are susceptible to harm could suffer grave consequences from a breach of confidentially. Ensuring culturally appropriate and context-specific precautions is crucial to preventing future hazards and harm to study participants.

3. **Risk Assessment:** During the research the researchers try to avoid harm usually. Harm to dignity i.e. not respecting person's right, physiological, social harm and informational risk are certain kind of harm which are to be avoided.
4. **Use of Vulnerable Populations:** Those people who are unable to protect their rights are called as vulnerable groups. The researcher can include vulnerable persons in the research after giving the justification for their inclusion. The consent from legally authorized persons or parents are required to conduct the research on vulnerable persons.

CHAPTER 19

Introduction to Consumer Protection Act

Introduction

Consumer protection is the practice of safeguarding the interests of the consumers. It tends to protect the consumers from the unfair market practices. It is the producer's responsibility to ensure that the commodities meet the needs and expectations of the consumer, but business people frequently fail to fulfill this duty and engage in unfair business tactics, such as adulteration and the provision of subpar products. So the Consumer Protection Act, 1986 was enacted to protect the consumers. The main features of this act are:

- This act gives consumers a number of rights and obligations.
- It provides safeguard to customers against malpractices of sellers and other forms of exploitation.
- This act provides a three tier redressal system constituting of district forum, state commission and national commission. At any stage, a consumer can file complaints in order to get justice.

Meaning of Consumer

A person, organization, or individual who buys goods or services for personal use is referred to as a consumer. They don't use it for manufacturing purpose or for the purposes of resale.

A consumer is defined as any individual who purchases goods or services in exchange for money and uses them for both personal and commercial purposes, including resale or commercial use, in Section 2 (7) of the Consumer Protection Act, 2019.

Importance of Consumer Protection Act

This consumer protection act is very wide as it extensively provides consumer protection at each step. It covers the rights, obligations, and range of consumer remedies. It is not just advantageous for customers; business owners should also take note of it. Entrepreneurs cannot thrive for very long by disregarding the needs of their customers. If companies wish to thrive in a cutthroat industry, they must give consumers the attention they deserve.

The importance of Consumer Protection Act could be described as follows:

1. Consumer protection provides information to all those customers who are aware and also to those who are unaware regarding the rights and remedies available to them. It spreads awareness by various means either through campaigns or by starting different programs, so that consumer become aware and shall start using their rights whenever their rights are being violated.
2. In order to run any kind of business, businessmen require some or the other resources of society. It becomes the duty of the businessman to use these resources for the benefits of consumers.
3. Although nowadays the consumer is recognized as the king of the market but then also there is somehow chance of exploitation of consumers as businessmen use various unfair trade practices to cheat and exploit consumers. Consumer protection act provides certain rights in order to safeguard the consumers from such exploitation.
4. The basic purpose of any kind of business is not just to create more and more customers but also to retain them. However businessmen can create more and more customers only by satisfying the demands of customers, protecting their interest and by meeting the current demands. Thus, as a conclusion one could say customers are the foundation of business.

Consumer Rights

Despite the awareness among the businessmen of their social responsibilities, the number of cases of consumer exploitation is on the rise. The Consumer Protection Act, 1986 provides the following rights to all the consumers:

1. **Right to Safety:** The objective is to protect consumers from the promotion of goods and services that endanger life and property. This right is essential to ensure a safe and secure life.
2. **Right to Information:** Consumers have the right to access comprehensive information about the quality, quantity, purity, standards, and pricing of goods or services, enabling them to safeguard themselves from unfair practices.
3. **Right to be Heard:** Where a consumer has been exploited or has any complaint against any product/ service then he has the right to advocate for his interest and be assured that his interest would be given due attention.
4. **Right to Consumer Education:** It is the right of consumers to acquire adequate knowledge and skills to be informed to customers.

5. **Right to Seek Redressal:** This right seeks to provide compensation and justice to consumers against any exploitation.
6. **Right to Make Choice:** Every customer, irrespective of their class or status is free to choose the kind of product he or she likes. This right grants every consumer the freedom to choose goods or services according to their personal preferences. Consumers are free to choose the most suitable product from their point of view.

Consumer Responsibilities

While the government and non-governmental organizations have made numerous efforts for consumer welfare, the success of these endeavors ultimately depends on consumers proactively safeguarding their own interests. Consumers must assume specific responsibilities, including the following:

1. **Responsibility to be a cautious consumer:** The consumer should not blindly trust the words of the seller. He must insist on getting complete information about the product.
2. **Responsibility to not to be carried away by advertisements:** The advertisement frequently exaggerate the qualities or features of a product or service. Consumers should compare the actual use of the product with what is portrayed in the advertisement. In case of any disparity, it is important to inform the sponsor of the advertisement and insist they stop giving misleading statements.
3. **Responsibility to insist on cash memo:** The consumer needs evidence of purchase to file a complaint, and the cash memo acts as evidence or proof that consumer has paid for the product or service. The seller is under obligation to give a cash memo even if buyer does not ask for it.
4. **Responsibility to buy quality products:** The problem of supply of substandard goods adulterated products and duplicate products can be solved only when the consumer himself stops compromising the quality of the product. Before making any purchase of goods or services the consumer must look for quality marks such as ISI mark, Agmark, ISO etc.
5. **Responsibility to file a complaint:** It is the responsibility of the consumer to file a complaint in case of any sort of exploitation.

How to File a Complaint?

In order to file a complaint, the following things should be kept in mind:

- Any consumer who has been exploited can file a complaint at any time within 2 years from the date of such exploitation.
- The consumer must possess the evidence or proof that he has purchased the particular product or service.

- The consumer must be aware of his rights and responsibilities.
- The consumer must have complete details of the seller.
- The consumer can file a complaint either through electronic mode, i.e., email or by filing an application before the court.
- The application can be filed before the district, state, or national commission depending upon the value of goods or services.
- The complainant must keep a record of all the documents.

CHAPTER 20

Introduction to Disaster Management Act

Introduction

The Disaster Management Act of (2005) is passed by the government of India with the purpose of efficiently managing the disasters and other aspects related to disasters. This law provides a basic plan and legal framework to minimize the impact of disasters on people, property and the environment. Mitigation, preparedness, response and recovery are the 4 phases of the disaster management act. These 4 phases ensure to combat disaster situations and provide a response in disaster events by giving certain kinds of assistance and providing other necessities to all those who are affected.

According to this act, disaster can be defined as any mishap, calamity or any grave occurrence that arises either due to natural factors or man-made factors resulting in loss of life, damage to one's health and property, degradation of the environment. Disaster management means a process of planning, organizing, coordinating and implementing measures in order to prevent threats associated with disaster, reducing risk linked with disaster, making things prepared beforehand to deal with disaster, helping to assess the effects of disaster to prevent it in the future.

Objectives of the Disaster Management Act 2005 (DMA)

1. This act gives federal and state governments the authority to create various other authorities at respective levels to reach the goal, i.e. to manage the disaster.
2. This act empowers the central government to develop certain preparative steps to mitigate disaster risk, consequences and effects in the affected area.
3. All the aspects related to disaster are covered in this act whether they be the relief measures or the mitigation methods.
4. Organize a financial aid for affected people and states.

5. Encourages coordination between various agencies and organizations in disaster management.
6. Encourages training and awareness programs related to disaster management.

Management of Disaster

- The Disaster management act has established NMDA (National Disaster Management Authority) as the apex body. NMDA will lay all policies and plans to manage disasters in India. These policies and plans are further implemented by District Disaster Management Authorities (DDMAs) and State Disaster Management Authorities (SDMAs) at the state and district levels.
- Disaster management plans are prepared by the government which includes complete detail of responsibilities possessed by various stakeholders, government agencies, non-governmental organizations (NGOs), and the private sector to manage disasters
- Further, the act mandates the establishment of the National Institute of Disaster Management (NIDM) and the National Disaster Response Force (NDRF). NIDM is responsible for providing training, research, and documentation in the field whereas NDRF is to provide specialized response capabilities in the event of a disaster. The personnel involved in NDRF are trained on certain aspects like as search and rescue, medical assistance, and evacuation.
- In general, the Disaster Management Act is an extensive part of legislation designed to provide India's disaster management system a legal foundation. Through the establishment of diverse agencies, programs, and standards, the Act seeks to mitigate the effects of natural catastrophes on individuals, property, and the surroundings.

The Following Governing Bodies are Established by DMA 2005

1. **National Disaster Management Authority (NDMA):** The chairperson of NDMA is the PM of India. All members of NMDA have a tenure of 5 years. The various policies are made and approved by NMDA and then to be followed by SDMA.
2. **State Disaster Management Authority (SDMA):** SDMA is headed by the chief minister of the state and includes 8 members who are appointed by the chief minister. SDMA prepares the disaster plan to be followed in their state and also follows the direction as given by NMDA if any.According to guidelines established by federal and state authorities, all state departments create disaster management plans.

3. **District Disaster Management Authority (DDMA):** The Collector or District Magistrate or Deputy Commissioner of the district is the chairperson of the District Disaster Management Authority (DDMA) and is responsible for preparing all the reports during any disaster. Also ensure that people are evacuated and all other basic necessities are provided to them.
4. **National Executive Committee (NEC):** This committee assist the National Disaster Management Authority at all levels. The NEC is composed of secretary level officers of government who are responsible for preparation of the National Disaster Management Plan. National disaster management plan which is to be followed by the whole country is annually reviewed and updated.
5. **National Disaster Response Force (NDRF):** It is led under the guidance of Director-General appointed by the Central Government. It is given the responsibility to respond to any threatening situation or disaster prevailing in the country. The Kashmir floods of 2014 and the Kerala floods of 2018 arc certain examples where the NDRF has played a great role in management.

Role of Pharmacist in Disaster Management

- Pharmacists are known for their work of checking prescriptions and for dispensing the drugs besides their role as mere dispensers, pharmacists also play a great role in disaster management. Broadly we can classify the role of pharmacist in disaster management as patient management, helping in response integration and provider of pharmaceutical supply.
- Pharmacists help to prevent the situation of panic and discourage among the patients by providing them accurate knowledge about dosage regimen and drug usage. Keeps monitoring the progression of disease and the impact of treatment.
- Ensures Response Integration and provides a continuous supply of pharmaceuticals by maintaining system of distribution of drugs under control. Also Co-ordinate with state and local boards in order to avoid redundancy.
    1. Recently in the COVID-19 pandemic, pharmacist played a crucial role in securing essential medicines. They achieved this by substituting medications with different strengths, opting for generic or therapeutic substitutions, and sourcing medicines from other countries or authorized suppliers.
    2. Certain additional roles are also performed especially during the absence of a physician like providing basic cardiac life support and cardiopulmonary resuscitation (CPR) functioning.

3. Some pharmacists do obtain a record of patients history and determine the medical condition of patients both before and after the disaster. Along with this, they have immense potential to educate patient about dosage regimens.
4. The American Society of Health-System Pharmacists (ASHP) organization promotes the active involvement of pharmacists in disaster planning. This includes the coordination of institutional pharmaceutical plans with private, local, state, and federal planners.
5. Further participation of pharmacists in policy making can contribute to disaster response effects.
6. Similarly, during anthrax attacks, the pharmacist helped the people by providing logistical support, i.e. pharmacist repacked and relabeled bulk medication for dispensing and then dispensed antibiotics to people who were at the risk of developing complications.
7. Community pharmacists functioned as primary care physicians in Canada in the year 2004 during the SARS pandemic. They performed diagnoses and provided prescriptions in absence of the physician. Pharmacies were kept open to help the patients despite the closure of emergency rooms. This shows broadening in the duties and responsibilities of pharmacists.
8. During the disasters pharmacist not only helps to dispense the drug but also transports the drugs to the affected area. For instance, it has been mentioned that pharmacists delivered medications even in the snow storm in the Washington.
9. Pharmacists are also regarded as toxicology consultants and poison specialists. They identify substances that are poisonous and provide antidote and therapeutic management information to physicians.
10. Whether it be a natural or man-made disaster that puts a devastating impact on the health of patients, pharmacists start taking on responsibilities outside of their usual scope of practice.

CHAPTER 21

Medical Devices

Introduction

India has one of the largest markets for medical devices across Asia, which is rapidly upgrading. Medical devices can be defined as any instrument, apparatus, software, or material used alone or in combination for the purpose of diagnosis, treatment and prevention of disease. According to WHO, medical devices include everything from computerized medical equipment down to simple wooden tongue depressors. Medical devices may include contact lenses, surgical lasers, pacemakers, dialysis equipment, baby incubators, medical gloves and bandages. The basic purpose for the use of medical devices is to sustain the life of and individual, provide replacement of any process or anatomical support.

Various agencies are responsible for the regulation of medical devices depending upon the area where it is being marketed or manufactured so different agencies across the world that are responsible are the US FDA (Food and Drug Administration), EMA (European Medicines Agency) and CDSCO (Central Drugs Standard Control Organisation).

Medical devices rule 2017 was the first rule related to medical devices that came into effect and it laid down risk-based classification of medical devices. In the subsequent year 2018, grouping guidelines for medical devices applications are applicable for the manufacture, sale, distribution or import license of medical devices. In the year 2020, amendments to the medical devices rules of 2017 came that provided classification of non-notified medical devices as well and illustrated steps for license application. As per the Medical Devices Rule 2017, medical devices may be defined as:-

1. "Substances used in vitro diagnosis and surgical dressings, surgical bandages, surgical staples, surgical sutures, ligatures, and blood and blood component collection bags with or without anticoagulant".
2. "Substances including mechanical contraceptives (condoms, intrauterine devices, tubal rings), disinfectants, and insecticides."
3. Devices notified from time to time under sub- clause (iv) of clause (b) of section 3 of the Drugs and Cosmetic Act, 1940.

Classification of Medical Devices

There are various ways to classify medical devices like on the basis of their intended usage, level of risk and other factors.

Level of RISK

Class I: Low-risk devices

The devices under this category don't have any effect on the well-being of patients and usually include those products that are at low risk. However during the manufacturing of these class products GMP standards are to be followed. Surgical dressings, alcohol swabs, elastic bandages and umbilical occlusion devices are certain examples of low risk devices.

Class II: Moderate-risk devices

All those devices that present low to moderate risk fall under the category of moderate risk such as X-ray machines, infusion pumps, and surgical drapes.

Class III: High-risk devices

All those devices that present higher risk to the patients upon their usage. Devices such as intraocular lenses, vein and thermal ablation devices, heart valves, and implantable pacemakers.

Class IV: Very high-risk devices

There are certain categories of devices that pose a serious risk upon their usage like those medical devices that are used to treat circulatory and nervous system disorders that may come in contact with sensitive tissues of the heart and spine causing a risk and thereby classified under class of very high-risk devices. Various other examples are: drug eluting stents, cardiovascular prosthetic devices, heart valves, deep brain stimulators and artificial pancreas systems. For high-risk and very high-risk devices, pilot trials are performed in order to evaluate the adverse events and effectiveness of devices.

Intended Use

Based on their intended use medical devices can be classified as diagnostic, therapeutic, monitoring or implantable devices. For eg:- the use a CT scanner acts as a diagnostic device which is used to generate a detailed image of the body whereas the use of an infusion pump acts as a therapeutic device and is used to deliver fluids in the body.

Basic Aspects Related to Manufacture and Sale

Both manufacturing and sale of medical devices are somehow a complex processes that involve stakeholders, manufacturers, distributors, healthcare providers and regulatory agencies.

Manufacture

1. **Design and development:** Manufacturing of medical devices starts with the designing and development of new products which involves intensive research and development, testing and prototyping. They should be designed in a way that provides safety and effectiveness.
2. **Manufacturing:** To ensure quality and safety of medical devices it is mandatory to conform to GMP standards at all time and to manufacture in a controlled environment only. All the processes shall be documented and validated to rely on the results performed and shall be analyzed through audits. The manufacturing will include assembly, testing and packaging.
3. **Quality control:** For any device to be marketed it need to meet the quality standards set forth by the regulatory agency.

Sale

1. **Marketing**: It is the duty of manufacturers to ensure that their marketing material is not misleading and their sales person are properly trained and educated about the selling product. Labels shall be clear and easy to read along with signs of warning or any other precautions. The name and address of the manufacturer should be clearly stated.
2. **Distribution:** Medical device manufacturers market their products to healthcare providers, customers, and distributors by various means either through advertising or by promotional activities.
3. **Regulatory compliance:** Records of all adverse events need to be maintained. Labels and advertising shall be as per the regulatory standards. Further obtaining a pre-market approval also comes under the regulatory compliance.

www.ingramcontent.com/pod-product-compliance
Lightning Source LLC
Chambersburg PA
CBHW071224230926
51849CB00001B/24